Norman Dugdale was born in Burnley, Lancashire, in 1921 and educated at Burnley Grammar School and Manchester University. In 1948 he moved to Belfast, where he worked as a civil servant until his retirement in 1984. From 1985 he was a member of the board of the British Council and was chairman of the council's Northern Ireland committee. Active in public life, he was chairman of the Belfast-based charity, Bryson House. A member of the famous Philip Hobsbaum 'Group' based at Queen's University, Belfast, Norman Dugdale published four full collections of poetry, *A Prospect of the West* (1970), *Corncrake in October* (1978), *Running Repairs* (1983) and *Limbo* (1991). He died in October 1995.

COLLECTED POEMS
1970-1995

COLLECTED POEMS
1970-1995

NORMAN DUGDALE

Introduced by Philip Hobsbaum

with a personal appreciation by Elizabeth Thomas

LAGAN PRESS
BELFAST
1997

Published by
Lagan Press
PO Box 110
BT12 4AB
Belfast

The publishers wish to acknowledge the financial assistance
of the Arts Council of Northern Ireland in the production of this book.

A catalogue record of this book is available from the British Library.

ISBN: 1 873687 45 1
Author: Dugdale, Norman
Title: Collected Poems 1970-1995
1997

Cover: *Portaferry Light* (1993) by Mary Dugdale
Cover Design: Kevin Cushnahan
Set in New Baskerville
Printed by Noel Murphy Printing, Belfast

Introduction

Norman Dugdale was a kind of character less often found these days than in the nineteenth century. He was a meticulous public servant who wrote lyric poetry in his non-too-abundant spare time.

Born in Lancashire in 1921, he was educated at Burnley Grammar School and went on to Manchester University, where he was an exact contemporary of the novelist, Anthony Burgess. Dubious health kept him out of the Armed Forces during the Second World War. Instead, he joined the Board of Trade in London as an Assistant Principal in the administrative branch of the Civil Service. He was transferred to the Northern Ireland equivalent, the Ministry of Commerce, in 1948, and spent the rest of his life in Belfast and its environs, rising by successive stages to senior rank in the Ministry of Health.

This meant, as can be seen from his literary work, that he was an adopted Irish writer. Irish settings abound in his poetry, and he has few equals as a topographical poet. The key to his writing is found in what may be his finest poem, 'The Disposition of the Weather', title-piece of an early pamphlet, and previous to that selected by Howard Sergeant for his magazine *Outposts* (Issue 69) in 1966. The poem begins:

My landscape turns to winter everywhere.
The seaboard stony, mountainous, is worn
By wind and rain as men are worn by time,
Bones sticking through the skin. Gaunt cliffs there,
Eyeless, towering Lears, confront the west
While the sea's hounds yelp and snarl about their feet.
By moss-grown chapels, Anglican, forlorn,
From Asia's heat the guardians rest
Of vanished empire—soldier, governor, judge.
Once upright sentinels their headstones lie
Stiffly askew: the houses they were born to,
Came home to die in and hand down,
Now carious mouths, gape at the sky.

Inland are bogs and lakes, some level pastures,
Few crops, no rich deposits in the earth.
Useless to mine or drill.

That most certainly is not Dugdale's native Lancashire. The Irish cliffs—"eyeless, towering Lears"—confront, not the choppy St. George's Channel, but the great breakers of the Atlantic swell. The hinterland does not comprise the wide cornlands of the Yorkshire dales, or the deep mineshafts of the English industrial north, but the bogs and lakes of a depopulated rural Ireland.

No Irish poet could have expressed that peculiar terrain in terms more appropriate. One thinks of Yeats and Kavanagh rather than Graves and Auden. But this is not only a matter of topography. The poem has a political edge. It is a matter of anomaly that Ireland, so heartlessly colonised, has supplied to the British Empire some of its most distinguished soldiers and administrators. In a masterly transition of imagery that takes us from gaunt cliffs to ruinous headstones, Dugdale reminds us that the cuirassiers of the Empire came home from whatever exotic climates of their administration to die in the icy wind and barren landscape of their native country.

A further transition moves the landscape into an allegory of life itself. The poem ends:

> And yet I know
> This is the disposition of the weather,
> Bleak and wild beneath all interludes; stands
> Henceforth in that quarter and will moan
> Wilder yet, round cape and reef, those islands where,
> Their features flattened by ten centuries,
> Blind saints who never knew a temperate zone,
> Gather my world into their world of stone.

The poem is in form a canzone, or extended lyric. Its lines are slightly sprung pentameters, but the rhyme scheme is not so formal as at first it may seem. For one thing, the three stanzas are of irregular length: thirteen lines, eleven lines and fifteen lines respectively. For another, no one rhyme scheme is followed through in each stanza. For a third, the incidence of pararhyme, as distinct from full rhyme, rises considerably towards the end. The form, in other words, serves a dramatic purpose—with, in the last stanza, "lure", "gear", "whether" and "where" part-rhyming and, in collusion with the increasingly sprung rhythm and chopped-up syntax, acting out the bleak landscape and wild weather which, allegorically speaking, is the poem's theme.

Indeed, this is a theme throughout Dugdale's work. Topographical poems include 'Kerry', 'Two in Connemara', 'Dublin', 'Belfast' and 'A Prospect of the West'. These are all good poems, and the last one named—title-poem of Dugdale's first (and best) book—almost equals 'A Disposition of the Weather' with its scenic exactitude and skill in matching that exactitude to an observation of life's struggle and passage. Here the sprung verse moves even further towards dramatic utterance:

> Now clear weather holds before the turning world
> Topples into winter. A few late bees
> Fumble the fuchsias flowering still in hedgerows.
> Peacock sunsets spread their purple glory,
> Foundering at last like galleons on fire
> Whose pennants stream at mastheads to the end.
> In dews of morning after early frost
> A full-formed rose gleams still; and axe-blade sharp,
> Great headlands splinter the unmoving sea.

The topography relates not only to Ireland but to Dugdale's native Lancashire. Here, however, he feels himself to be an exile. Consider such poems as 'Haven Street', 'Downham Revisited', 'The Farther Shore', all in *A Prospect of the West* (1970), and, from *Corncrake in October* (1978), 'Dalesmen in Craven', 'Hurstwood', 'A Winter Journey'. The voyage is through time as well as place. In the last poem named, he has returned for his mother's funeral:

> Now, from windy Ireland struggling home
> Through lashed airports, black turbulence of cloud—
> Shap blocked, the roads a quagmire—I have come
> Too late. Ice fumes the windows of the room
> In which you lie, your frail flag struck, the siege
> Slow-mounting, ended in this brutal sack.

The speaker's present domicile, Ireland, may be windy, but 'home' is a place of utter repellence. In a late poem, 'Apparition', he speaks ruefully of being called a foreigner by an Ulsterman who has been alive for a shorter time than he himself has dwelt in the Province. If there is a parallel, it may be seen in the naked thew and sinew of his language, which in moments of anger resembles that of another exile in Ireland, Hopkins.

The weather usually seems to be bleak and the terrain forbidding in Dugdale's poems, but this in its turn relates to a theme that inexorably came to dominate his writing. *Running Repairs* (1983) is a book overshadowed by its author's failing health. This matter is dealt with in terms of a characteristic dry humour: "lying high and dry in hospital" ('Mason'); "we settle to the strict routine/Of their impersonal compassion" ('Back to the Basics'); "A hunger-striker/Rattling in vain its gaunt contracting cage" ('Age'); "Brakes worn,/

Tyres frayed, the steering wobbly and the road/Dropping ahead"
('Pantechnicon'); and the title-poem itself, retaining the metaphor
of a worn-out vehicle:

> It won't be much of a job, you understand—
> Simply a makeshift minor op.
> Under a local anaesthetic. Certainly
> Things won't be any worse, and given luck
> They should be better.

If a little more prosaic, the later pieces are refreshingly crisp and
witty. They are underpinned by a lifelong preoccupation of the
author: the poetry of the Ancients both in Latin and Greek, and also
the modern Greek author, Cavafy. All Dugdale's books are
interspersed with allusions and translations, and the epigraph of his
final collection, *Limbo,* in fact has an epigraph from Cavafy: "Always
you must have Ithaca in your mind./Arrival there is your predestined
end". There are references to and versions of Cavafy in earlier
volumes—'The Last Alexandrian', 'Theodotus'—and a really superb
translation called 'In a Large Greek Colony: 200 BC' in Dugdale's
final volume, *Limbo* (1991):

> That things aren't what they should be in the Colony
> There remains not the slightest doubt. Possibly—
> For all that we edge forward still somehow—
> The time has come, as not a few think now,
> To bring in a political reformer.
>
> Yes. But the snag, the difficulty
> Is that they make such a self-righteous fuss and stir.

Compare this with the work of other translators, even good ones
such as the American, Rae Dalven—"There is not the slightest
doubt/that things in the Colony are not going as desired"—or the
Englishman, John Mavrogordato—"That things in the Colony are
not going to perfection/Not the least doubt bears inspection".
Nobody can question the knowledge of Greek exhibited by Dalven
and Mavrogordato; it is the quality of their English verse that is in
debate. One version of Cavafy is prosaic, and the other at times
downright ugly. The note on the subject that Dugdale himself has
supplied gives evidence of the care with which he approached his
text, and incidentally bears witness to the deep consideration that
he gave in all his poems to questions of craft and technique. Other
translations, and also some welcome additional poems—'Half-

x

Remembered Things', 'Prelude', 'Scrapheap', 'Rue Lepsius'—may be found in the appendix of new and uncollected pieces at the end of this edition.

Norman Dugdale rose to be Permanent Secretary of the Ministry of Health in Northern Ireland, ironically struggling with his own health during most of that time. He continued to live in the Province after retirement, and died in Belfast in 1995, aged 74. His accomplishments as a Civil Servant are a matter of public record, and were particularly notable in seeking to bridge the long-standing sectarian gap between the Protestant and Roman Catholic communities. His poetry has continued to appreciate in the minds of the discerning. His was an exquisitely tuned voice, mastering form and content alike. Norman Dugdale was not afraid to confront the grimness and depredations of life. He had at call the poise, and, beyond that, the stoicism which his Greek, Latin and Irish mentors had taught him.

Philip Hobsbaum
1st January 1997

Founder of the Belfast 'Group' of poets in the 1960s, Philip Hobsbaum is a poet and critic. He currently lectures at the University of Glasgow.

CONTENTS

Introduction *vii*

A PROSPECT OF THE WEST
(1970)
One and Many *3*
Personal Appearance *3*
Kerry *4*
Anglican Church: West Cork *4*
Two in Connemara *5*
Dublin *6*
Belfast *7*
Persephone *8*
Swift *8*
Louis MacNeice *9*
Lines for an Old Lady *9*
Landfall *10*
Pennines *11*
Easter in Craven *12*
Haworth *12*
Haven Street *13*
Reasons of State *15*
Downham Revisited *16*
The Farther Shore *17*
Tourist Season *18*
Great Portland Street *19*
Pavane for the 'Forty-Five *19*
For Better For Worse *20*
Poor Fitz *20*
The Disposition
   of the Weather *22*
Frontier Incident *23*
To Venus *24*
Queene and Huntresse *25*
Perseus *25*
Galatea to Pygmalion *26*
Nocturne *26*
Retrospect *27*
Against Abstraction *27*
An Enemy *28*
A Narrow Place *29*

On a Recent Happy Event *29*
Prospect of the West *30*
Evensong *31*
An Exorcism *33*
Sea-Change *34*
A Question of Identity *34*
Single Ticket *35*

CONCRAKE IN OCTOBER
(1978)
Prolegomena *39*
Bog *41*
Anarchist *42*
Some Notes
   for Impartial Observers *42*
Salmon-Leap: Co. Mayo *43*
Fire Risk *43*
Autopsy
   on the Fourth Decade *44*
Marches *45*
Disciplinary Case *45*
Definitions *46*
Self-Portrait *46*
Northern Spring *47*
Clerk's Tale *47*
Seated King and Queen *48*
Lares *48*
Aubade *49*
November Afternoon *49*
Littoral *49*
Waste *52*
Proper Names *52*
Problem Family *53*
Recluse *53*
Place and Time *54*
Back Water *54*
All for Hecuba *55*
Nekuia *55*
Night-Ferry *55*
Terminus *56*

Remembrance
of Things Past 57
A Study in Sepia 57
South Mancester Revisited 58
Peripeteia 58
Corncrake in October 58
Dalesmen in Craven 59
Hurstwood 60
Not in the Brochure 61
No Second Troy? 61
Apocalypse 62
Dolphins 63
The Last Alexandrian 64
Scheria 64
Scholar Emeritus 65
Thasos 65
Ithaca 66
A Winter Journey 67

RUNNING REPAIRS (1983)
Theologian 73
Spirit of Place 73
Columkille 74
Lent 75
A Statement
is Expected Shortly 76
Visitation 77
Pantechnicon 77
End of Season 77
Provincia Deserta 78
Back to the Basics 79
Quis Multa Gracilis ... ? 79
Souterrain 80
Pillar of Society 80
Candles 81
Journeys End 81
Polycrates' Ring 82
Michaelmas 82
Home for Christmas 82
Grief 83
Mason 83
How to Become
an Alexandrian 84
High Hodder 84

But for Your Gifts 85
After the Bombing 86
Travelling Westward 86
At Saul 87
Scholar in the Library 87
Trivia 88
Second-Hand Bookstall 88
To an English Liberal,
Ten Years On 89
Encounters 89
In Memoriam G.B. Newe 89
Age 91
Diplomatic Reception 92
Shipwrecked Mariner 92
Specimen 93
Daybreak 93
Glenarm 94
Small Hours 94
Theodotos 95
Running Repairs 96
Moralities 96
Silence 98

LIMBO (1991)
Shrouded Coast 101
Donegal 101
Elder Statesman 101
Robin Among
Summer Visitors 102
New Management 102
School Photograph 103
Tryst 103
Tynan 104
Long-Distance
Coach Station 104
In a Large Greek Colony:
200 BC 105
Inner City 106
Final Act 107
Hallowe'en 107
Lovers 107
Homage to the Bard 108
Cretan Mantinada 109
Age 109

Progeny *109*
Talking Head *109*
Leader of Men *109*
Old Man Sitting
  in the Park *110*
Natural History *110*
Trading Station *110*
What's Wrong
  with Aberystwyth? *110*
Pre-Retirement Course *111*
The Commissars Confirm
  their Short List *111*
Age of Heroes *112*
Ribblesdale *113*
St. James's, Piccadilly *113*
Mr. Cavafy's Byzantine
  Archon Versifying
  in His Exile *114*
Last Night *115*
Medizers *115*
Crossings *116*
Polonius Complains *117*
Satan's Advice *117*
Staff Party *118*
Olympic Games *118*
Apparition *118*
Insomnia *119*
Metamorphosis *119*
Celtic Bard,
  Burgher's Wife *120*
Remorse *120*
Gerousia *120*
Domestic Interior *121*
Overture and Beginners *121*
The Other Kingdom *121*
Zoo *122*
White Church at Ballintoy *122*
Limbo *123*

New & Unpublished Poems
(1991-1995)
Half-Remembered Things *127*

Young Man and Old *127*
A Toast *128*
A Memorial for My Sister *129*
Closed Shop *130*
A Woman of Nazareth *130*
Camouflage *131*
Ballymacarrett Blues:
  Summer 1994 *132*
Ancestry *132*
Prelude *133*
Scrapheap *133*
Shoreditch *134*
Medical Ward *134*
Sunday Service *134*
Maker *135*
Rue Lepsius *136*
Man of Property *136*
Rector *137*
End of the Affair *138*
Five Cretan Mantinades *138*
Lower Order *139*
Planter *139*
Harvest *140*
Epiphany *140*
Christmas Eve *141*
One of the Boys *141*
Landscape in Winter *142*
There are More Things *142*
The Roundabout *142*
Aunt Sissie *142*
Family Tree *144*
Beginnings and Ends *145*
Afternoon in Early March:
  East Belfast *145*
Sea and Stars *145*
Absentee *146*

Personal Appreciation 147
Notes to Poem 165
Publisher's Note 166
Notes & Index 167

A PROSPECT OF THE WEST
(1970)

'and he a middling kind of a scarecrow, with no
savagery or fine words in him at all'
—J.M. Synge, *The Playboy of the Western World*

ONE AND MANY

Lord, let me now and then forget
The bag of bones I lug round yet,
And save me from the absurd I
Who haunts these poems like a spy
In multiple disguises, shifts
That cannot hide the inner rifts.
And may I learn that good is not
Sprung elsewhere, but pitched in what,
Here and now, this common light
Reveals. So, by gifts of touch and sight
Walking my world, may I pass through
All false identities to grasp the true:

PERSONAL APPEARANCE

He strides in from another world, this man
Of fifty, lean survivor from
A decade out of fashion with the young
(Spain, the hunger march, the League, the pogrom).
They watch him guardedly, lest they succumb
To fame or charm, ready to detect
The slightest sleight of hand or slip of tongue.
In muddled middle-age among all these
Untouched as yet by time's perplexities,

I note the strength concealed in his repose—
Grey hair brushed back, a swarthy face, hooked nose,
Wide mouth twisting upwards at the corner,
Hands resting on his knees: the whole effect
Remarkably Roman, as of one endowed
With ruthless energy for love or war.
When he begins to speak a rasping, loud,
Commanding voice confirms the metaphor.

After the reading there is generous applause—
And yet I notice they remain unwrung

By what most moves him—then some questions, then
Leaving the warm and lighted lecture-room
We shuffle out into the mist and gloom
Of the November night. 'Frankly'—
Some golden Pyrrha, turning to her friend—
'I wasn't terribly impressed.' 'O, I don't mind
His poetry, but his teeth are yellow.'

They think of him as someone left behind,
Signalling vainly from a past now dead.
I think of him as one gone on ahead,
Deeper and deeper in the wilderness

And finding his cipher clear I realise—
Alone now, walking along streets I know—
I must have crossed the frontier long ago.

KERRY

Here Ireland thrusts a great arthritic fist
Into the Green Atlantic, and a dying life
Moves with the grave slow rhythm of the waves
Expiring on the tremendous beaches. Among
These bogs and stony fields, the peat-smoke
Acrid in the dusk, only the tourist
Prospers, with his camera and car
Bringing the lure of cities to the young:
Destroyer of old truth, old faith, old tongue.

ANGLICAN CHURCH: WEST CORK

A surprise, after the slap and suck of tide,
Salt spume, sun-dazzle of the estuary,
This weathered roof and spire, old spars that ride
Here in a creek of time, folded from the sea.
Drunk on foxgloves, glutted with musk-rose,
Bees weave a drowsy silence round the close.

I mark the decent plainness of squared stone:
No soaring pinnacle, arches that strain
Upwards, but measure and proportion
Resisting shake of wind, the rot of rain

Through centuries, its bulk and girth
Rooted in these few yards of racing earth.

A decent plainness too within:
No fretted vault, carved architrave,
Saints writhing in contrition of their sin
Or splendour of stained glass in choir and nave,
But seemly all, comporting with the rite,
And gathering through clear windows light.

Almost at the world's end witness to
The lucid statement of dark mysteries,
The church of Swift and Taylor, of the few
Under the nettles here and dancing bees:
The susurration of encroaching sea
All these blent voices, whispering through me.

TWO IN CONNEMARA

I

This business man whose affable 'Good mornings'
Bespeak a hearty breakfast is like Crewe
Or any main-line junction thousands pass through,
Pausing only to change trains: full of smoke
And stir, announcements, rumblings,
But also useful information, comforts, things
Such as no traveller should despise—
Times of departure, destinations, tea,
Fags, paperbacks and news. Even in his guise
Of solitary fisherman he makes a crowd,
Bulky, jocular, derisive, loud.

II

The poet wears his fame as carelessly
As some old jacket baggy from long use,
Smiles, murmurs, nods to all; but being courteous
And grave by nature cannot wholly shed
The formal elegance of his address,
Transporting to the emptiness
Of bog and mountain, water, stunted wood,
His burden and his gift, the solitude
That guards his conversation with the dead.

DUBLIN

Autumn blusters in the square. Squalls of rain,
Scudding before a strong south-westerly
Across Kildare, spatter my window-pane
And set it rattling high above the street.
There on his pillar gull-stained Nelson drips,
Staring beyond the porter-laden Liffey
For signals from a long-since foundered fleet.

And there, investing Christ Church and St. Patrick's,
Grim forts held by a shrunken garrison,
Swarm smoky tenements, the huddled bricks
Where the city's poor lodge tight and multiply
Their kind. But shadows of the beaten dead
Stalk this town still, or crowd across its sky.
I think especially of one who fled,

The broken dreamer of a pastoral dream,
Of one out of his mind, another torn
Between his duty and desire. They seem
With Essex, Mountjoy, Wentworth, only lately gone.
Now dowagers totter in decayed hotels
Who once looked out on half a county; and wind
And rain no shutter bars or roof repels

Plunder their rooms at will and nettles grow
In houses envy gutted or their sons
Consigned to browsing cattle and the crow.
The hidden workings here of history,
Running like unmapped mines beneath the land,
Cracked the foundations, wrenched everything awry
And out of true that my kind meant to stand.

Shored-up, and fissured so, this city now
The devious Gael commands but cannot quite
Possess, embrace the queen or disavow
The harlot. To me her raddled grace,
And breath infused with whisky, stout and gin
And watery eye suggest the sort of place,
Late-rising, boozily hospitable, that might

Afford a leaky shelter now the days draw in.

BELFAST

City of gull-flecked gantries, cloudy city,
Raised by steam and iron from mud and marsh,
God-ranting, canting, pious without pity,
Pillaged by gales, marauders that swarm
Out of the tempestuous Atlantic,
Trudges at daybreak, caps and dungarees
Over the bridge, wharves by sluggish water
That slops and flops its tongue against the quays,
Men in thousands moving through the murk,
Shapers of ships will cruise on cobalt seas
Elsewhere.

Now cranes are still, clangour of steel
Suspended in the evening's sultry haze.
The smell of porter seeps through alleyways
And bits of garbage float with scum and oil,
Turning with the tide. Down reaches smooth as foil
The sirens of departing steamers
Echo from shadowy, sea-bird plaintive shores;
And slippered women issue from their doors,
Gathering at street corners with the dusk
To chat in curling-pins and aprons, call
For straying children.

All stridency of day
The moon dissolves, revealing a blanched crone,
Confused by wrongs, troubled by old resentments,
Her memories hugged round her like a shawl,
Muttering and mumbling through the dark.
And bonfires blazing on waste lots to mark
King Billy's triumph, James's overthrow,
That cast their shifting shadows on the night
Of bogeyman and hero long ago—
Dried faggots these of ancient rancour still
Smouldering in her heart and there kept warm—

Splutter and sigh, and one by one die down;
Turn into signals of distress
By lost survivors kindled on some shore
Glitter of moon and sea's indifference drown.

PERSEPHONE

Although it cannot last,
This shock of sharp delight
The blind heart craves and chooses
That everywhere encounters you
In lanes embanked with blue
Violets and dog-roses,
These hedgerows fuchsias' flames
Run like wildfire through:

Although it cannot last,
This rock of pulse, the flush
And ripple like a race of tide
Through tranquil waters ruffling wide,
Tug of wrist divining you
In February's sleet and slush,
Among black flowers, a marguerite
Umbrellas jostle in the street:

Knowing it cannot last
Sears so; but how should this abide
Or any ecstasy
Against the rub and grin
Of the greasy world outside
Or that fault fissures all,
The sudden shift or fall
Of the fractured world within?

SWIFT

Dread like a storm-cloud from the start
Massed in his mind, purpled, sagged and hung
In molten menace. The slow death then of hope
Marbled him, with fleas and pygmies shut
Forever in a famished Lilliput
To suffer there the slower death of heart,
This Gulliver in chains whose monstrous head
Flashed inner lightning as the darkness spread.
To plague him still, Court flies—those clegs on dung
Each summer stirred to frantic life—buzzed their brief
Erratic dance of pomp and vanity.
Mere starving gnats that bit him till he bled

And they grew drunk upon his blood, the Irishry
As ever he despised but fed: chafed
In smoky Dublin, sodden Laracor
Under the carapace of scorn and pride
While friends fell silent, loves he had denied
Unflowered in their violated dust.

                              Still
The calcined heart that would not give him rest
Drove him, drove him, trudging the inchoate
Moon-cold landscape of despair
His madness lit, the crusted craters there
And choked black furnaces of his charred skull.
In slag and clinker, ashes of ancient war
Only his stumbling carcase had survived
(Whipped by serfs, battered by grief too late)

The blaze of mind went out that warmed the poor.

LOUIS MACNEICE
Buried at Carrowdore, Winter, 1963

Alone in the keen air a hawk swings wide
Between the sea like steel and the lough's fanged shore
Of shining rock salivated by the tide
And rakes the famished fields round Carrowdore.
Stiff yet with frost, the numbed earth hardly stirs
Through days of drought, soil's drought and drought of heart,
Ebbed season when the angry sun strikes spurs
On ice in vain or sulks in mists apart.
Soon, though, spring will come inching in, to brim
These creeks, fill silent woods with song at prime—
Mindless music he will never hear
Who over the wintry landscape of his time
Soared solitary, over the charred, grim
Stumps of cities, tundra frozen in fear.

LINES FOR AN OLD LADY

So they are all to go, then—church,
Gaunt bastion of the straitened faith
Victorian wealth and piety

Piled on these slums a century ago
To guard an Orange enclave in the Green;
The drunken alleyways that lurch
Against its sides and brawl about its feet,
Hugging their quarrel close; each crumpled street
Seething with cats by night and kids by day—
All are to go, in one great swathe
Scythed flat to make an urban motorway

And speed the suburbs into town. And this is right,
For all have served their turn and time. Now traffic's
Rising drumroll shakes the porch, flicks
Mortar loose and rumbles deep within.
The terraces like elderly bronchitics
Cough in their smoke at dawn: at nightfall wheeze,
Propped back to back and riddled with dry rot.
And phthisis eats through lungs. So let
Fire burn, bulldozers pulverise the lot—
Pews, common privies, poverty, disease,
Compounded in the dust.

                    But what then should
The unconsenting heart, itself
Grown rickety at last with age
(That rooted in blind reasons has withstood
The sour constriction of this place
And by some miracle of grace
Reaches still to light and leaf)
Do, but shrivel in such rational cold rage
To rip and batter all, and all for good?
Where else should it strike home? How put on then
The crooked glory of unlooked-for Spring
Or under its spread of memory seed again?

LANDFALL

Stiff-gaited, cumbersome, the great steel bird
Waddles to the airfield's edge, stops, suffers there
A shudder of sudden power, then lunges, lifts
And leaps, cloud-cleaving, clear into radiance,
Over the masked earth, seas and cities
Soars in seeming freedom, though curbed still,
Responsive yet to skill of hand and eye.

Despite the nubile hostess, neat in nylons,
Dispenser of charm and reassurance,
This is man's element, where risks are real
Yet calculated, the rush of chaos
Resisted by a wafer: marvellous
The thrust of mind sustaining this machine
Athwart a toppled sunset, under cold stars.

Then stoops, slithers once more through cloud. Suddenly
The city glitters in the depths below
Encrusting with innumerable jewels
The plain black velvet of the countryside.
Swings and sways above, engines cut back,
The huge wing gently scything swathes of light
While in their comfortable suburbs sit

Millions for whom the weather of the world
Is only a diagram on a screen.
So trundles to a stop on windy tarmac
Among mechanics, smells of kerosene,
Coaches, hoardings, neon-signs. We descend,
Resuming shabby lives with satisfaction
Or relief, and disperse in the wilderness

Our sharp, synoptic vision shifted, blurred
By this magnification of the night.
Earthbound, I plod parched country now,
The crumbling mass and muttering decay
Of Dis's gloomy kingdom: unredeemed unless
Some spirit singing here in time's duress
Conjures a clear spring yet beside the way.

PENNINES

Mere bacilli the diesels crawl below
On twisted roads wound tight between
Smudged towns—clamped
Like crabs in the intestines of these hills.
Huddled under the smoke, a people here
With little expectation labours still:
While over the bull-necked, empty moors
In summer larksong soars, arching the silence
With intricate fan-vaulting everywhere.

EASTER IN CRAVEN

East wind gnaws the fells, rubs
The white scars raw of limestone crags,
Tugs at trees, picking the skulls
Of sheep last winter knifed: nags
This northern land like toothache still.
But look, the air is luminous.
By crannied wall, crouched farmstead
First crocus thrusts, then daffodil.
The waters move beneath the earth;
The great limbs stir, tumbling bells,
Toppling gravestones, shaking the dead
In every dale. With crash of rocks,
Stiff banners blazing, Christ stands forth.

HAWORTH

First through the comfortable cotton towns—
Burnley, Brierfield, Nelson, Colne—whose pubs and clubs,
Co-ops, Marks & Spencers, bingo-halls
Manumitted thousands throng, released by Saturday,
Ignoring the wayside pulpits' tattered warnings
Outside the stone-faced chapels of Dissent
That gathered soot and silence with the years:

Then by the road that reels about the moor,
Heaving up heights, staggering beneath
Stiff stride of pylons straight across the sky line,
Round the sheep-farms crouched beside their drystone walls,
On a cool summer's evening I have come
Where the parson with the strange unYorkshire name
And delicate, pale children came, among
Booths and Ackroyds, Holroyds, Sutcliffes, Hirsts.

I park the car and get out and look round.
The museum is closed, the trippers
Have nearly all gone home: hikers and bikers,
Bright in their shirts and blouses, who have left
No sense of gaiety behind. A torn poster
Flaps on a gable-end. Dead flies
Shrivel in empty shops. It might be any
Stone-built Pennine village, struggling glumly here
To keep a lodgement underneath the moor,

Not hostile but indifferent still
To strangers, such as these were. One drank,
The others did not mix but gave no trouble.
Soon, genteel-poor and riddled with T.B.,
They guttered out like candles in a storm.
No need to gape. The place is in my bones.

But as dusk falls and a rising night-wind
Rustles the few trees, I shiver and am glad
To turn away, beckoned by lighted valleys
Whose colours flash like fairgrounds, loud with the din
Men make to frighten time, the lurker in the dark
Beyond the warmth and flicker of their fires.
Here, in spite of the guide-books, postcards
And biographies, alien, unappeased the dead
Endure in silence and the curious
Find no welcome.

HAVEN STREET

I

Uncle Henry always wore his cap indoors
On top of a knitted woollen helmet which
Covered his ears and chin. He used to say his
Face was bad; and right enough it twitched at times,
Whether from neuritis or some other cause
I never knew. He had watery eyes, skin
Trout-grey, hands and nails ingrained with dirt although
They hadn't twisted warp for many a year.
And whenever father put jobs in his way
(Which he did from time to time) Uncle Henry
Used to send word his ear was bad, or turned up
Only for a day, then crept off home again,
Thin, worried, pale, to hide from draughts and nurse his
Lot, crouched by the near-dead grate, and put the blame
On Norman or MacDonald and the Tories.

II

Aunt Bertha was his wife, my father's sister.
Childless, they lived in a four-roomed terrace house
On Haven Street, together with Aunt Annie,

Father's other sister, who wasn't married
And always stayed at home. Somehow Aunt Bertha
Managed on their dole; patched, darned, scoured the Co-ops
For bargains, kept the place neat, sent cross-words in
Sometimes to *Tit-Bits* or *John Bull*, never won.
In old age she reminded me, with her plump
Hands, plump wrists, the dimpled smile that lit her plain
Round face, of Rembrandt's mother without the ruff.
But that of course was later. Whenever we
Visited as children (which wasn't often),
Aunt Bertha beamed at us, pressed us to bread, tinned
Salmon, tea. We pecked and shuffled, looking glum,
Yawned, the horse-hair sofa pricking our bare legs,
Daunted by dingy gaslight, their adult talk
Of small calamities among the neighbours
And cancer and T.B. Mother sympathised
As always. Father fidgeted, his restless
Mind pawing at such constraints.

                    And all the while
Aunt Annie, upright in her chair, rocked gently
To and fro, jingling her pendant ear-rings with
An air of languor and disdain. Aunt Annie,
You see, was a ruined woman. She'd demurred
When Father offered to set her up in some
Small business—dress-making, perhaps a shop. That
Would hardly have been genteel or suited to
The care and sympathy so clearly due
To one in her position. Indoors or out
Aunt Annie couldn't quite bring herself to work.
We nippers were scared of her, she seemed so grand.

III

After the War—my father dead, Aunt Annie
Too—my wife and I called once or twice, newly
Married. His stammer worse, Uncle Henry hid
In his corner, trying to conceal the white
Bristles that spiked his chin. Aunt Bertha, beaming,
Told us about my father as a lad—how
Mathematics hoisted him out of the mill:
How he filled a drawer with silver, kept it so
For everyone to help themselves; came home then
At all hours, whistling, up again by five. But I

Looked like my grandfather, she said—tall, thin, one
Shoulder high. She gave us some plates, her mother's
Best, unused for sixty years. Back at the flat
We rigged them up. Within a month they fell, smashed
Irretrievably. Aunt Bertha had no luck.
Then one day we heard from home that she was dead—
A fortnight later, Uncle Henry too, a
Hundred pounds in notes stuffed underneath their bed.

IV

Sometimes now I sit in my office and I
Think of Haven Street. My carpet runs from wall
To wall; fresh flowers grace a side-table; thick
Velvet curtains reach down to the floor—the faint
Click-click of a typewriter the only noise
Obtruding through a sound-proofed door. Such timid
Gentle creatures, they waited with the patience
Of the poor, a lifetime almost, fed on scraps,
To die. And even my father lost heart at
The end—the War, his absent sons, a stroke, his
Mounting disabilities. A childless man
Whose genes lift his left shoulder, whose bloodstream bears
The family's transmissible diseases,
I pace my crumbling hereditament, scan
The entail sealed in darkness, stamped in bone; try,
Forty years too late, to make amends, piece by
Piece assembling what I find as best I can.

REASONS OF STATE

Mostly the butchery occurred elsewhere.
Someone was knifed among the shadows or
Garrotted at the dark turn of the stair—

A scuffle and groan, blood on the walls and floor,
Then silence. The courtiers smiled to hide their dread,
Being frightened of the truth and even more

Of being known to know. Though rumour spread
King kept his secrets, Council held their tongue
But thought it seemly they should mourn the dead

And quietly discouraged those among
The foreign embassies and fools who tried
To pry into the facts or right the wrong ...

Half-crowns paid for entry, we join the guide
Or wander round in summer frocks and flannels,
Stare at the portraits stiff with ruffs and pride,

The armour, faded tapestries, enamels.
Inside, the rooms seem cramped and dark, lit by brief
Shafts of light, revealing the dust on panels

Sprung with damp or age. Emerging with relief
We start up children's games or make for tea
At tables on a terrace, we whose chief

Virtues are domestic, who disagree
With violence, tend our gardens, knit, provide
Against the future and do not think to see

Such evil in our world. Somewhere inside
The labyrinth men shift and calculate,
Huddle together where the ways divide

Or grope and stumble through the fog of hate
(Mouths choked with dust, eyes straining) long for ease,
An end of torment, treachery, debate,

Who murder innocence beneath the trees.

DOWNHAM REVISITED

Cold, witchered country this I walk today,
Seeking myself. A slim hawk hurtling there
In March's mad contention rounds to stay
And wrestle the rough wind, boisterous air
The dog snuffs, ears blown back. The brows of fells
Are vizored still with ice that blocks a slow
Spring struggling through the lanes, relieving dells
Where daffodils are shivering in snow.

Beside the church, from their long ache of bone
The dead await release, obstructed by

Millstone grit and clay compounded with limestone.
I read their names, who moulded all I see.
Perilously now rooks build; roots long dry
Stir here in earth exactly defines me.

THE FARTHER SHORE
'tendebantque manus ripae ulterioris amore'

Heysham slides past the window, once again
Materialising slowly through the dawn,
Roofs scurfed with frost, streets empty still. Here & there,
A patchwork of pink and blue beside the line,
Lights snap on in curtained bedrooms where
Men blink and rub their jowls and women yawn,
Untwining curlers. After the night at sea
I recognise my own again, this country

That I took for granted once, and thought I knew
By heart; that now, familiar and strange
Seems always out of reach when I pass through.
Again this morning as we cross the Fylde, then slow
Through Preston breakfasting in mid-December fog
And frowstiness, I search for landmarks from the train
To lead me back through my barked world, restore
The rub of its first timber and true grain.

These journeys sometimes curve into illusion, then
Swerve hard back to reality—as when
I watched old shires (sheer miracle in May)
Out of the gnarled and rooted centuries
Stubbornly flowering still, like canvas whirled away,
A stage-set in the dusk; or swinging free,
Some great cathedral ride the moon's floodtide
That lists next day, a silted argosy

Beached, barnacled with age. Such beckonings
Out of the past are tricks of light, not things
Either my father or his father knew.
Their England jolts into my view
O, on any fine Spring evening that I share
With figures in a landscape (such as, here,
Some city like a monstrous starfish stings
And thrusts its poisoned salients into)

Whom twilight has reprieved: a baby
In its father's arms, waving to the train,
Shirt-sleeved men, smoking in their allotments,
A couple strolling on a cindered lane,
Hand in hand. Or else it glimmers in the night
Through clots of steam, whisps and rags that drift
Down platforms where a few late travellers stand,
Wan faces drained of hope beneath the lamplight.

I think of them, those generations then
Entombed among the millions of men
England mangled or devoured, whose catafalques
Are these charred cities smouldering everywhere,
Incinerating time, that spout and flare
Through fissured crusts. Too late I reach
Towards lives I almost touch, they seem so near,
Yet now recede from, faster every year.

TOURIST SEASON

Buttocks like balloons squeezed in their chairs,
Thighs plumped tight as pre-war sausages,
In bulging middle-age these burghers sit
And sweat and swill and guzzle: from Europe some,
Some from America and some
My fellow countrymen, on holiday
With false teeth and unsmiling faces.

Outside, in the white glare of midnight,
Walk the young of many nations, vaguely
Excited, hoping that something will happen;
Or they sit on the steps of public monuments.
But nobody lives here any more
And they have all come to stare at each other.

Upstairs are a dozen storeys
Of lawful embraces, snores, seductions,
Slamming of doors, flushing of lavatories,
Farts, eructations ...

If Rome was anything like this,
Do you wonder that Horace preferred his farm
And his vines and the cool Bandusian spring?

GT. PORTLAND STREET

Caught in the undertow of memory
I am drawn back and back

And find myself again where this began
(O long ago) beneath the arc
Of lamplight like a spread-out golden fan
With faint mist thickening towards the Park
And the trains rumbling underneath my feet
And not much changed—except that no-one comes
And I am fat and bald and ridiculous.
The thing died years ago: why make this fuss?

Pale ghosts climb slowly from the Underground
In ones and twos, and go their Sunday ways
With dismal faces. A tired old crone
Under the booking clerk's indifferent gaze
Stands clutching a sack, grateful for warmth and light.
Not much changed? I come in from the night.
It all looks shabbier now and meaner.
Shabby and mean, and shrunken in the dry, stale air
I buy my ticket and descend the stair

And gaze along the empty platform. Well,
I think I will return to my hotel
And read for half-an-hour and so to bed.
Better go quietly when all is said.
Yet I could rage with Herod, or blubber
Like a boy, to think that leper's breath
Infects her too which poisons me to death.

PAVANE FOR THE 'FORTY-FIVE

They are shadows all, cloudy presences
Looming like mountains through the mist
By loch and sullen moor—that prince
Who thought French manners, gaiety and dash
Would fetch the burghers as they charmed the girls,
The clansmen vaunting in their pride who had
No plan but plunder, vainglory, revenge,
A cobwebbed cause which glitters briefly still,

Spangled in early dew, then snaps,
Dissolves into this rainswept desolation

Where the touring heirs of Cumberland,
Sundered here from cities, sealed
By safety-glass in coach or car
From spattering of guilt, the stain of blood,
Fidget for the telly or *The Times.*

FOR BETTER FOR WORSE

Assured of my inheritance—
Great mansion, rich demesne,
Gardens elegant, formal, trim,
The art of Italy and France—
A lolling heir I spent my days
In idleness and wit and laughter:
For wealth and honour would come after
As summer ripened the green fruit
And you fulfilled the promise of your gaze.

In a garret now above a slum,
Arthritic fingers bent around my pen
(Those cynical remarks upon my elders!)
I scratch in vain and scratch and wonder when
In this anonymous mean place
You last showed me some favour, some
Hint of recognition. O ageing Muse,
Encumbered by an ailing poet,
Why do you thus avert your face—

To hide the ravaged glare would strike me dumb?

POOR FITZ

Died as he lived, an apostate; was burned
    Without the benefit of clergy,
Flowers, music, prayers one Saturday—a few
    Colleagues at hand, to do their duty.

Outside, January roared its grief,
    Lashing the graves. We filed out one by one

Numbed in spirit, numb with cold,
    Sprinted for cars, our duty done.

Later, warmed by whisky in a snug,
    'Queer chap, old Fitz. A wasted life.
Strange that he never married. Well, lunchtime.
    Best get back home to the wife.'

Next week his personal effects
    Were put away. A brisker man
Sat at his desk, despatching files
    Poor Fitz had kept, a ponderous gnome—

Big head, round belly, short, thin legs,
    The deep, slow Limerick voice—
Lumbering behind events, for ever
    Questioning that, considering this,

And making cumbrous jokes about his name
    And family heritage and pride
That brooked no compromise. It struck me then
    He meant it all. Lived as he died

In scorn of pliant men who'd rather
    Bend than break: gave what was due
In honour forty years, took nothing back
    Except the means of holding to

His passion for astronomy. What folly
    Or madness made him fix his mind
On shadows so?—the abstract truth
    A loadstar for whose sake he dined

Always alone. O yes, a wasted life
    Compared with ours, who have promotion,
Car, kids, wife, and watch each other out of eyes
    That meeting, slide into evasion

Or signal sly complicities.

THE DISPOSITION OF THE WEATHER

My landscape turns to winter everywhere.
The seaboard stony, mountainous, is worn
By wind and rain as men are worn by time,
Bones sticking through the skin. Gaunt cliffs there,
Eyeless, towering Lears, confront the west
While the sea's hounds yelp and snarl about their feet.
By moss-grown chapels, Anglican, forlorn,
From Asia's heat the guardians rest
Of vanished empire—soldier, governor, judge.
Once upright sentinels their headstones lie
Stiffly askew: the houses they were born to,
Came home to die in and hand down,
Now carious mouths, gape at the sky.

Inland are bogs and lakes, some level pastures,
Few crops, no rich deposits in the earth.
Useless to mine or drill. There age by age
Generations wither, poverty endures—
Together men and beast inured to dearth—
Like rock beneath thin soil. And now the wind
Has settled in the east, stripping the trees
Before their time, breathing ice on pools,
Blanching field and hedgerow. A tattered thorn,
Waving its ragged arms about the sky,
Warns of the weather still in winter's horn.

One day no doubt the wind will back and veer,
Heralding rain. Brief anguish of the spring,
Blossom and leaf, will pierce the land, recalling
Lost springs elsewhere. Summer perhaps may lure
The Spanish trawlers once more with their gear
To anchor in the bay at dusk (the moth-winged,
Warm, almost Iberian dusk), their hands
Sprawled at ease on deck. And yet I know
This is the disposition of the weather,
Bleak and wild beneath all interludes; stands
Henceforth in that quarter and will moan
Wilder yet, round cape and reef, those islands where,
Their features flattened by ten centuries,
Blind saints, who never knew a temperature zone,
Gather my world into their world of stone.

FRONTIER INCIDENT

I

That day the first rumours reached the City
Of a disaster somewhere to the north,
The wall broken, the eagles lost,
Some till then tranquil, unremembered province
Burning. But nothing changed. Trains ran to time,
Traffic filled the streets. At the airports
Visiting celebrities arrived with smiles
And statements for the waiting pressmen.
Each week-end parks and pleasure grounds were full
Of people strolling in the sun.

              Later
Survivors appeared, in ones and twos,
A handful only, were cared for,
Found suitable jobs, but moved henceforth
Like sleep-walkers, sealed in their appalling vision.

II

Of course there were rallies, counter-attacks.
Brave men, devoted men, kept the system going,
Gave their lives in battle or at the desk.
Yet gradually dikes and frontiers crumbled,
Dock and nettle sprouted through paved streets,
Roads reverted to mud, commerce to barter,
Well-tilled land to waste.

            While ministers at court
Bickered or wept or intrigued out of habit,
While distraught millions in the metropolis
Rushed in panic through the streets, rioting
For peace, or prayed for some miraculous
Deliverance, and bands of mercenaries,
Drunk and deserting, started to rape and loot,
The last of all the line of emperors,
Sword in hand, at a breach in the ramparts
Died, calm eyes fixed on the enemy.

TO VENUS
Horace, Odes iv, 1

Not again, O surely not again, dear lady;
I pray you, do not disturb my peace again,
Not after all these years. I am not what I was
When that cheerful girl Cynara reigned

But am getting on for fifty, after all,
And have almost forgotten the drill—those
Stern commands your lisping sons convey.
Shouldn't you be visiting love-lorn lads elsewhere?

Or, if you want to cause a proper stir,
Why not make a formal progress, swans and all,
In your full regalia, drawn by purple swans,
To the portals now of Paulus Maximus,

That brilliant young lawyer—handsome, eloquent,
Accomplished—whose clients dote on him? (They buy
His tongue but cannot buy his heart.) Your standard
He will carry far and wide, triumphing everywhere

With flutes and laughter; and by the Alban lake
He'll set your marble statue in a shrine
Of fragrant wood, and there for your delight
While clouds of incense swirl into the air

And the small pipe plays its descant to the lyre,
Fleet-footed youths and maidens twice a day
In Salian time will dance beneath the shade
And magnify your greatness in their songs.

As for me, I have no zest for contests now
Of wine or love: no longer bind my temples
With the new season's flowers or entertain
The slightest hope of a requited passion.

Then why should I be tongue-tied when she comes?
Why should her image trouble my dreams so,
Elusive phantom I pursue in vain
Among the Campus Martius' alleyways

At dusk and through the fields? If she should vanish
All will go dead within, or worst (far worse),
Empty years stretch out while underneath
The thickening crust the sterile fires still burn.

QUEENE AND HUNTRESSE

You define my world; bring
Into focus everything
The night obscures; reveal
The shabby shifts that make up me
And simply by being you,
So freshly minted, bright and true,
Expose the grubby counterfeit
That passes here for currency.

Glimpsed only through your cloudy veil
Pacing above, you silence all
The grunting rout in this gross sty,
Circe's swine, that kick and brawl,
Compact of envy, malice, gall,
Moon-struck now: among whom I,
Who stumbled on your nakedness,
Tremble for that discovery.

PERSEUS

Somehow it must be done. Clenched will
And muscled arm were not enough, he knew;
Such simple attributes, for all his skill
With spear and sword-blade, would not see him through.

Even with aid of Gods he could not face
In hell's murk what waited for him there,
But only through obliquity of glass
Confront the writhing snakes, withstand that stare.

Must then in a sweat of horror hack
With eyes averted, slithering in blood,
Rip the dripping head-piece from the neck
And scrabble with his burden through the wood.

The exploit had its uses, he would learn,
Calm later and considering—the tale alone
Would silence disaffection, the head turn
His enemies into astonished stone.

Felt play of air, sun warm upon his skin,
As petrifaction slowly spread within.

GALATEA TO PYGMALION

Now my blocked mouth is loosed. My eyes
Through marble's veined opacity
Swim into light: breasts, shoulders, thighs
Break surface, rippling the stone.
Out of mute matter, clogged obstruction,
Dragged by your urgent hands I rise.

Sea-sparkle, dance of wind and sun
Among the leaves, dazzle me still.
Brine tingles on crushed lips, my tongue
Tastes the salt earth, whose each deft thing
Wounds and delights me—stumbling
Still through this bright world I venture on.

You turn away, repelled to see
Your once pure marble a botched creature,
The breached, sacked citadel so lately
Stormed by your lust. Yet I assume
Gladly what you shrink from, would disown,
Your inmost self fleshed, every flaw, in me.

NOCTURNE

Tangled in gantries still, a struggling moon
(That sidled over mudflats on the shore,
Slipped past sheds, fingering freight
On puddled quays) inches up the windy sky.
Now, last buses leave for depots with a roar
That dribbles into silence. Late cars
To laurelled suburbs swishing home, wink
Round corners, vanishing in spray. Now only clocks
Possess the town, leaning over roofs to pry

At lovers in their doorways, shuttered bars,
Or tall as cyclops, each with one fixed eye,
Stalk drink-befuddled sailors back to docks.

Now mind unclogged runs clear at last, emptied of
Day's clatter and the clutter of the day.
I walk the streets mobs bullocked through,
Butting and mauling in the blind affray
Of Green and Orange with their god-crazed eyes,
Despair and rage at riot in their blood,
Here, out of sight, you took your slender rise,
Through all the press and trample of the crowd
Frail and inviolate; and hidden still from view,
Past midnight now you circle somewhere home.
But look, from every wisp and whorl of cloud

The moon steps free, scouring rooftops white,
Cascading through stone chasms, silently
Flooding the fronded city with salt light.
Among the symbols of your plenitude
Through all the glittering forest spread
And coral glades, lone traveller I move,
Your incandescence blazing in my head.

RETROSPECT

Ares and Aphrodite snared
In fine-meshed verse: to catch these
Was to be his compensation
But the great gods broke the net with ease.

He patiently retrieved his gear
And limped away, resolved to trawl
Elsewhere for fish of rainbow hue.
Plain cod and hake: his meagre haul

Rots daily on the harbour wall.

AGAINST ABSTRACTION

Miles don't matter—
    By the score, few or one,
    They come to this, that you are gone.

And more than distance time
    Divides. A moment, like the Fall,
    Here or elsewhere, shatters all.

How mean these fears.
    I snatch my little good
    And hoard it from the multitude

While you, whose bounty
    Shames me so, set out
    Waving a gay good-bye to doubt,

Are lost among
    Restless millions blown around
    Like tickets on the Underground.

Unlike that girl
    Velasquez drew, of earth and fire
    So compacted that desire

In the beholder yields
    To contemplation of stillness
    Past all repose or reach of flesh

We change, but only grow
    By striking deep. Such spread
    Of leaf and blossom overhead

Declares you rooted so,
Grounded here, no matter where you go.

AN ENEMY

Converting your base metal into gold
Would cost me no small labour. I refrain
Partly from sloth, partly from conviction
That there are better things to do, but chiefly
Because we stand together on the same
Doomed raft, swirling into the dark.

A NARROW PLACE
Ieu sui Arnaut, que plor et vau cantan.

I have pinched and scraped, sulked too long
Shuffling all these grimy years among
The mean black streets and crooked alleyways
Of my constricted heart; have grubbed about
Its garbaged gutters for stale scraps
To eke my destitution out.
The dole affords a man no sense
Or expectation of magnificence.

How then could I know, how guess
That out of the squalor, smoke and mess,
The narrow ginnels, you would rise
With your soft mouth and grey-green eyes,
My phoenix-girl, and clap your wings
In joy; and by this miracle assert
Your true descent—not out of common things
But the high lineage you bear from kings?

What it devours it yet makes new
This conflagration in the dark
Of bird and bush and living tree
That as it blazes blossoms too
And sears and scorches, scouring me:
By which, with perfect clarity
Eyes long accustomed to the murk,
Undazzled, unamazed, now see.

That ruin rings this festival, I know,
But move here into settled night
My dread consumed all in delight,
Rejoicing, love, yet weeping too
That I, whose rotten makeshifts time leaks through,
Seeps within and spreads still like a stain,
Have only rags to shelter you
And keep your frail hands warm in the cold rain.

ON A RECENT HAPPY EVENT

That clammy toad with popped
Green stare and palpitating chin

Who squatted at table, belching, blown
So tight he could not budge

By sliminess has slithered, flopped
Into preferment: swells, a judge,
To our amazement and his own.
Ermine, wig conceal his grin

Shovelling flies and harlots in.

A PROSPECT OF THE WEST

After the sudden spring, wonder of earth's waking,
Stir of wild things in the woods at dawn
About the sleeping house, all day in elms
About the rooks' indignant clamour, summer failed us,
Turned wet and cool, with cloud upon the hills,
A blustery wind persisting day by day.
All we had hoped for then we somehow missed
Which others seemed to gather and enjoy;
And not the unregarded moments only—
Blue brilliance of mornings, sunlight splashed
Beneath the planes about the cobbled square—
But grace of growth and gaiety and ease,
The long, hot season nourishing the seed
That strives towards fulfilment.
                                    So summer passed
Unnoticed almost till its end drew near.
We cut our sheaves, garnered the meagre harvest
And hid our disappointment from each other
In silence or in talk of other things.
Now clear weather holds before the turning world
Topples into winter. A few late bees
Fumble the fuchsias flowering still in hedgerows.
Peacock sunsets spread their purple glory,
Foundering at last like galleons on fire
Whose pennants stream at mastheads to the end.
In dews of morning after early frost
A full-formed rose gleams still; and axe-blade sharp,
Great headlands splinter the unmoving sea.

What's then to come? At evening down the lane
A whistling lad brings news of distant wars, unreal
Calamities, the cries of time-trapped men

Enacting their delirium of gall
And greed and lust. All's steady yet, no stir
Or flicker from the weather lurking here
Below earth's rim. What gusts, though, gashed,
Smashed the gull and wrung the shag's fine neck,
Honed down to bone the saints in their stone cells
Who shivered at their prayers along this coast
And groped for mercy through the gale? What terror
Did they know, what shelter find here from
That whirlwind outside time but sticks and straw?

EVENSONG
'He hath scattered the proud in the imagination of their hearts'

I

Mist-fall, leaf-fall, the plane trees flare
Like torches, showering gold: leaf-fall, dusk-fall,
Settling now to sharp October night
With streetlamps wreathed in fog
And swirl of faces under yellow light,
The confident eye, uncertain smile
Looming and vanishing.

Now bearded youths
And foolish virgins in 'phone booths,
Lodged against the windows, grin
Down mouthpieces at unseen dates.
Women bulge with shopping bags,
Shoal in supermarkets, nibble stalls,
Nudge homeward, groceries gathered in;
And pub doors swing by dockyard gates
Spilling dunchered men and din.
The city stretches, contemplates
Its long weekend. The pleasures beckon
Of Friday night and Saturday,
Fags and booze and fornication
Which Sunday drowses, belches on.

II

Slops through the window from the street
The drumming life that roars below

And eddies down the ward. Here in neat
White rows as in a catacomb we lie
Entombed in our failed bodies. Each
Confronts alone another night
Of antiseptic smells and sweat
And whisperings by dim blue light,
Ebbed, slack hours when doubt and fear
Spread like mudbanks, looming clear
Of day's receding tide. One by one
We gather on the shore
As souls upon that stagnant reach
Who wait for the grim ferryman,
Palms black with obols, to appear.

III

Three-o-clock. Life everywhere
Contracts into its inmost keep,
Beleaguered, sapped, as out
Of hiding places cold winds creep
To occupy the town. In ragged bands
They loot the bins, whirl scraps about,
Rattle rotten windows, blow
Across the derelict decades,
Pocked, scarred wastes abandoned to the slow
Attrition of corrosive years
Where memory shoots random flares
Ripping the dark, and on the wire
The insomniac in silhouette
Twitches, mouthing, staring yet.

What treasons hidden in the blood,
Heart's abjurations, have betrayed me,
Dismembered here?—bones, hands, feet
Strewn through the city street by street
Or scattered in the river's mud
With rusty cans and old spitoons,
Cracked-voiced Orpheus whose head croons
Still the perils of the night,
Unheard. Now may it drown
Under the snores, the drunken sleep
That stupifies this brawling town.

IV

But lighten at last our darkness.
As blotchy dawn with smoke-sore eyes
Peers through blinds, fumbles sheets
And underclothes on chairs, may
Mind struggle up to consciousness
Heaving the body from the crumpled bed;
And cranes like herons motionless
With lifted beaks along the shore
Strike at barges, buses, streets,
From our fragments framing day.

AN EXORCISM

The thick blood smokes. Fend off those shades,
That woman in her scarlet dress,
That muttering man. I would not hear them. They
Pre-figure what they cannot say.

Let others drink. See, these are froth.
A drop revives them and they fall
To cards, coquetry, scandal, snuff,
Dallying so with silken stuff

They have no time to prophesy.
Leave them be. That flesh drips down to bone
And lipless mouths no longer kiss—
Their squeaky chatter comes to this.

But that man shoulders through the throng,
Stoops at the pit, lips darkening.
Begin, begin then, since I must
Parley with your raging dust.

The mournful treacheries that roosted in
Your riven heart, like ravens in a keep,
Flap here in mine, craws crammed with carrion.
Your tale's foretold. But, speak; have done.

SEA-CHANGE

What laughter stirs him, couched
In sand and leaves, that wanderer
With salt-encrusted limbs, the sea-chafed eyes,
Who rustles like a lion in the brake
Shaking off sleep? Bursts forth—
What sack and pillage, spoil
Of cities, mangled men, confront the cool
Slim girl among her squealing handmaids? Crouched
At her feet, what cry of bone for rest
Craves parley here? For soothing oil,
Her supple hands, the knotted sinews ache.

But needle drags him north,
Tide pulls, no matter what the haven.
Slips from her arms into his element
That howls about him, homing through the night
Towards a son unfathered, an old man
Sonless, memory gone, and wan
Penelope, dozing by candlelight
Who sweats in nightmare, seeing him heave
(Those twenty stiffening years) his girth
Ashore, the bloated dead
Heaped on his back like barnacles, and weave
Segmented thighs, the bulging, hairless head,
To make a havoc of his hearth.

A QUESTION OF IDENTITY

I surface slowly, sink, rise, sink
Again. 'He's coming round', a low
Voice says. I'm coming round then. 'Who
Are you?' Three faces, indistinct,
Hover above. I try to think—
My collar's off, my shirt's undone,
Sopped in sweat—and focus on
A tablet set into the wall
Which names a benefactress. So,
That's where I am. Who am I, though?

Well, I used to be myself. I wear
My clothes, of course—that tie is mine,

This jacket too: support my wife,
Open my letters, sharp at nine
Drive to the office. You might say
I'm oiled by habit, strict routine,
Domestic, mated, middle-class,
The sort of cog worn frictionless
By use, that spins the whole machine.
Only, it's not me who leads that life.

No. Nowadays, there's wild uproar
Within. Caliban floors Prospero,
Ariel raves. All stagger, snore,
Slumped in a heap, till you restore
With syringe and needle, deft, cool hands,
A truce among my brawling glands—
As if just now I'd strayed into
The Quattrocento and you three
Were Botticelli's Graces. My
Name? My occupation? Certainly.

But you are still anonymous
In white starch, your separate selves
Doffed, bleached out, intent again
On your next patient while I fuss
With tie and collar, assembling this
My compound ghost, as best I can;
To stumble out into the rain,
Indexed, filed, on the record
In triplicate, my fissures shored—
Towards what further precipice?

SINGLE TICKET

To a flutter of flags and handkerchiefs
We step into the huge arena,
Sacrificial victims, who wave in turn
Towards faces penned behind the barricades.

Some with foreboding watch, some with grief,
But most from curiosity, here to fill
An idle afternoon with buns and tea,
The thrill of possible disaster.

These we disappoint, climb clear and cross the coast.
Ships like slugs trail their white slime
In and out of Liverpool; and slowly clouds
Slide shut below, rolled in by the Atlantic.

We chat and smoke, cocooned in noise and comfort,
Who smell still of the miles of mouldering brick,
The millions lodged there underneath the grime—
Heading for gull-screams, granite, silence.

CORNCRAKE IN OCTOBER
(1978)

*The Corncrake ... is seldom seen, being very secretive in habit ... It is usually
concealed in long grass, and is also semi-nocturnal ...*

Notes. A harsh 'crek, crek', which may be heard at night as well as by day.
                                    —The Observer Book of British Birds.

PROLEGOMENA
for John Smith

Evanescent, thin as smoke, the cries
Of Tristan and Isolde curl
Across the open window where
Like St. Simeon Stylites
Beside a classic portico
You perch contemplative in air.
The Rolls and Bentleys prowl below,
Slinking through alleyways to pounce
Upon the clamour of the stage
And sleek to suburbs with their prey
Of diamonds and cigars. Now
The Opera House clangs shut.
Only pigeons strut and flounce
Among the cabbage-stalks to play
Their small ironic comedy
That's of this place though not this time,
With peck and pout and flutter mime
The polity of civil bow
And cards and coquetry and snuff. See,
They conjure ghosts—from Drury Nell,
Sparks from Bow in tattered silk, the shy
Professor and the flower-girl meet
To dance about the empty Garden
And down the length of Floral Street.

Such whimsies, though, are not for you
Or for your time. The backward glance
Is fatal on high wire. Your stance
Needs nerve and skill, disdaining stunt,
The comfort of a safety-net
Or headlong dash for home. And yet
Not for show or for applause
These aerobatics but because
High wire's the shortest way
To cross the smoking falls

And Thunder of your Niagara.
Well, I've no head for heights. I keep
A strict terrestrial motion still
By sweat alone, and envy you
Your easy gait—in all you do
A true civility, good sense
Like 18th century decorum
Town-bred, but of the country too.

So, each day by four
Or five o'clock the fruitful earth
Pours riches at your own front door
With apple smells, the smell of grape
And pear and peach. Shy poems knock
From printing-press or office-block
Limping in from drought and dearth,
Or licking sores about the mouth
Like beggars out of casual wards
Crave nourishment, the truth
And sparkle of your exact words.
And thence made whole, set free, depart
Among the fevers of the street
To work their healing art.

II

Here the dominant idiom's
Lowland Scots, not Gaelic—scouring
As caustic soda; spiky as whin
Guarding its ground against encroachment;
Bitter as nicotine, chewed plug
Squirted from the corner of the mouth.
It scalds the ear, red-hot steel
Plunged hissing into water.
You handle it with pincers, bang
The rivets home, every stroke
A wince and jar for wrist and brain.

Not then in Horatian ease, sunning
Myself upon a competence
In middle-age, but in a hole
In no-man's land among the random flares,
The stubborn maul of butting mobs
That bellow in the mire, I learn
The use of poverty: to sift

An acid soil that nurtures only hate
With wild dog-roses twined in every lane.
Such shafts as Heraclitus shot
Out of his fiery mind were barbed
With brilliance to pierce the dark. These
Are calibrated on a scale
Less cosmic—the smoke and sweat
And squalor all transmuted if,
By small exigencies of rhyme,
The crude ores fuse and the alloy
Rings true, and of its place, and time.

BOG

Black contusions bruise the frame
From Mizen Head to Malin. Bog
Drags all the middle down. From Cork
To Donegal the roads crack

And stumble, ploughshares tilt
Into its tufted maw,
This spread throat gulping rain,
Slurping it up like porter

Day after day. The old soak
Sinks the lot, with toothless gums
Stuffing its fibrous gut,
Masticating bird, man, beast,

Worked chalice, jewelled cross—voids
Nothing for millenia. Come Spring
And Spring's dry easterlies the spiked
Gold coronet of whin

Crowns a vast necropolis
Whose tremor of chthonic force—
Septs sunk in spongy earth,
The seepage of their sodden wars—

Confounds all reckoning by sun
Or star as turf-smoke drifts,
Blue bitterness at dusk, and cabins
Kneel in clusters to the dark.

ANARCHIST
'Canst work i' th' ground so fast?'

Sapper, snorting under sleep, furiously
Detonating smooth suburban lawns: small
Sharp-snouted saboteur, subverting all
Appearances—I know you only by
Your random ruck and havoc, hugger-mugger
Sweltering below. You knock off with a grunt
Somewhere to snore the day-shift out, your stint
Ended in bleary light before I stir.
Suppose some neighbour stumbled on you, though,
At summer's end, curled tight in leaves and clay,
Where would you scurry, squinting thickly through
Those torpid eyes? Lie deep, then, while I trudge.
Rummage where instinct guides or luck. You dredge
The darkness still that irrigates my day.

SOME NOTES FOR IMPARTIAL OBSERVERS

Flown over, it is a conurbation
Much like any other: docks, sheds, sidings;
Traffic coiling through its gut; high-rise blocks,
Half-built estates spattering the country round.

Lived in, it is a minefield triggered
By invisible trip-wires. Wayleaves by day
Give access to some common zones, where the inhabitants
Frat cautiously, ears cocked for trouble.

By night, it drops all civic pretension
To assume a true plurality. Each warring village
Stands to, mobilized against the stranger,
Its strong points pubs, back alleyways its fields of fire,

Binlids radar. Take comfort, though. The hatreds
Generated here are locally consumed. Thus,
Regulated by the surgeon's knife, the rituals
Of decent burial, the economy

Registers near-perfect balance. You may expect, then,
A polite, if bored reception: to find your glittering
Goodwill irrelevant as a moon-shot,
Your advanced views (so thoughtfully designed) mere junk.

SALMON-LEAP: CO. MAYO

This sliding world—the lick
And trial of weeds, shadows
Pooled like oil—with lazy flick
They glide through. Then under
The weir, white ruff of water
Cartwheeling in its thunder,
Recoil like guns and flash
Their ranging shots whose arc
Falls short, smack on stone. Or thresh
In file up gullies, storm
The parapet and sink,
Black torpedoes locked
On target, zooming home.
It seems all things succumb
To June's carnality,
Even this ancient
Bony land where hedgerows
Run in spate with splash
Of iris and dog-rose
And fuchsias scorch the path
Beside the stream.

                    Old man content
To loll here while the salmon
Burn, flailing to fulfilment:
Old dog stretched in the sun
Nuzzling a flea,
What's to comfort you when, spent,
They drift back to the sea?

FIRE RISK

Behind the squared-off, plate-glass thoroughfares
These tenements in alleys serve their turn
Still, with shadeless lamp bulbs on the stairs
And creaking hoists and brown linoleum
And cockroaches in corners where the loos
Fizz suddenly and gurgle in the gloom.
But drop a fag or a light or blow a fuse
And woosh—up they go, the funerary urn
Of partnerships-at-law, old ledgers, bills
And last year's calendars on dusty sills.

Which is why, at my age, one shouldn't play games
With matches. Considering the lumber stuffed
On every floor, the fabric wormed from hall to loft,
The slightest spark could send me up in flames.

AUTOPSY ON THE FOURTH DECADE

No call, you think, for panic yet
Though putrefaction like a stain
Spreads within. Mind's plod, the stink and sweat
Of body, trudging the mill,
And then the rumble night and day
Of subterranean argument—
The same ramshackle rolling-stock
Recurring like an Inner Circle train
Jolting through the tunnelled dark
And peopled platforms of the brain—
Such classic symptoms need no skill
In diagnosis. Let's say
The rock-base hardens, cools. A temperament
From the start inclined to be obsessive
Tilts steeply into age.

                    Just so. But some
New shadow blurs the negative.
This blotch here that darkens the X-ray
Disturbs, like a fuzzed snapshot of the Falls
The morning after a riot—
Smashed streets, smashed lives, the drunken vomit,
Stunned silence settling with the pall of dust.
Focus this then. Now you come
To consciousness: know what crawls
In the palpitating viscera whose spasm
Convulsed the face the shaving glass affronts
With smoke-shot eye and stubbed chin today.

MARCHES

After dark, it is best to keep moving—
Not too fast, for the roads
Wriggle through hills, slithering past hedge and ditch,
And the next bend may conceal a few stray cows
Or a blown bridge or ambush. But if you can,
Keep moving, headlights drilling the night.
For these causeways cross an ancient wildness
And you are certainly being watched
By unseen eyes, the mild beasts
Helpless and indifferent in the fields.
Fix your eyes on the tunnel of light
Churning ahead. Menace enough, the moss-green
Drip of roof and wall, the ivy-throttled trunks
Flailing at you as you pass, blackness
Closing like a thunderclap behind you.

Not that the gutted towns invite a pause
Where doors are slammed on strangers. Pass through.
At the end of your journey lies home. There
For sure your coming is expected: though
By whom, this pelting night, you do not know.

DISCIPLINARY CASE

Reading the file from front to back (the wrong
Way round, I know, but it was late at night)
I assumed he was a brash young man, boasting
About his girl and his impending marriage
And now he needed leave to show her London
And anyway was too well qualified
For such a routine job. It came as a shock
To find at last he was 57
With a history of severe depression.
Ah well, he isn't the only poor old bugger
Working here with fantasies more apposite
To youth. I let him off with a warning
To settle down to his bread and butter,
And the silent wish that another chap
I know, not far behind and kicking still
Against the pricks, would also take the message.

DEFINITIONS

I

Lust first—the common itch
Of gut and groin, caught from
The strong contagion of the ditch
All scratch and squelch in, dog or bitch.

What's love, then? Love's the name
Of a like itch but worse, that burns
And barks and tetters the whole frame—
Not cured by scratching, all the same.

II

No matter what terms mind may coin
Arrowing into space,
In the end it all comes down
To what the body says

Whose vocables are brief and blunt,
Accidence stripped down to norms.
But from such shifts, by cry, by grunt,
Love's basic syntax forms.

A SELF-PORTRAIT
Ugo Foscolo: 1778–1827

Face, brow, deep-scored; sunken eyes that burn
In pallid cheek beneath pale hair; bold
Nose; lips full and firm, quick to curve in scorn,
Less quick to smile. But then the ape takes hold—
Thick torso, matted chest—shambling in my old
Patched suit, bandy-legged. I shrug and turn
My back upon the mirror, as the world
Its back on me whose monkey-tricks I spurn.

Melancholy mostly, at times morose,
Not given to hope or fear; by fits and starts
Clown, courtier, peasant, hermit, knave;
My speech is rational, but my heart's
Black ventricles, blood-crammed, in darkness rave.
Death, you will bring me fame, and give repose.

NORTHERN SPRING

Whins blaze along the coast
From Fair Head now to Fanad—
Gold-hoards glittering
In rath, in dun.

The bay in winter still, I climb
Clear of shadow, marvelling
At blackthorns in their bridal dress
And violets in the ditch and primroses,

Small trumpeters of resurrection,
On either bank. It is the whins'
Fierce shout, though, lifts the heart, war-bands
Rallied here against the sap

And siege of time: their sudden
Glory seaming gullies, haloing the hills.

CLERK'S TALE

Suddenly this morning Autumn's slow
Smouldering damp ignition bursts in flame
Along suburban avenues.
Cupped in black branches plane-trees glow
Like braziers, dropping cinders with a dry
Patter on the pavements; and kitchen flues
Brown the curling edges of blue sky.

Late stragglers at request-stops queue
Like random flies, arrested thus
Among the smoke and crackle of their days
Some shining moments webbed in dew:
Then shuffling forward one by one,
Each to his declension,
Grip the rail and mount the bus.

SEATED KING AND QUEEN

The wind intones its rumours through their heads,
Out of the febrile cities of the south
Carrying report. They give no sign,
Eyes void, their hands at rest, whose sovereignty
Is shrunk to rock and water, this citadel
Of beak and claw. Yet not in defeat
They wait, unmoving and unmoved,
For stars in circuit to fulfil their reign
After the thunderclap of fire, the scorched
Millenia of silence when—
Winding from what sunken Troy, past caves
That delve into the legendary dark—
Slow tribes shall come to clasp their feet again.

LARES

What need have you to ring the bell
Backwards in a muffled peal
Of mourning or regret? The small gods
Whom you serve—those deities
Of hearth and store—have served you well
Through garnered years. Upon your coasts
No storm-cones fly. Under a kindly sun
Among your spread of golden corn poppies
This autumn splash vermilion.

Considering the strata lie
Tilted north, how mean the soil, and thin
And bitter still the wind, no wonder that
My tillage here is slow to fructify,
Stubborn in its yield. Yet not this
Want of metamorphosis
Grieves me now. It might have plagued me once,
God knows. But not these mornings when,
A step beyond the door, feet slither in

Night-blood congealing on the stones.

AUBADE

The stab-wound on the skyline bleeds
To candid rose, unfolding wide
Across mudflats. The estuary
Crinkles with the rise of tide

Scouring scum, opening the stiff
Hinges of the city's rusted heart
And clanking ventricles to spurt
Salt life within. Now buses jerk,

Red corpuscles down clotted streets
Where suburbs cough to consciousness. In sewers
And alleyways rats slink to sleep. Soon bombs
Will suppurate to burst like sores

Spattering pus and hate, while bees today
Through all the murmuring miles of Ireland
Rifle the blue distance thick
And musky with the scent of may.

NOVEMBER AFTERNOON

Rock ribs the foreshore at low tide. Gulls
Squawk aloft to squabble over small
Pickings in the sludge. A sour wind
Slouches off the lough, with knife in hand
Skins children's faces hurrying home
From school: spits now at passers-by
Hurrying through unaccustomed streets
In faded light, head down lest
Some stranger stop them, murder in his eye.

LITTORAL

I

On a rock or reef, this spit of land
Hardly a foothold anywhere. Below
The trampling islands buck and strain
To drag their tethers in the bay,

Foam running from their jaws; or blow
Like whales, blunt heads butting the north,
Oiled backs sluiced by gouts of spray.

All day, a hulk adrift the house
Has wallowed in the gale. Now
A door slams somewhere in the dark
As round the great turf fire the talk
Through whiskey and tobacco haze
Runs on trout-streams, politics and law.
I yawn, nodding agreement. Yet
The scared cur cringing in my clothes
Pads through pools of silence, rubs its snout
Against blurred windows, whimpers at the shout

And havoc of the wind. Heads down,
Their pelted faces trickling rain
Under black sou'-westers of storm cloud,
The mountains haul the cabled road
That whips and writhes between us and the main.

II

Croagh Patrick like a tonsured monk,
Bald head circled by a fringe of cloud,
Ponders the moonlit missal of Clew Bay
Whose crinkled blue and silver curls
At the edge where small waves crisp the shore.

No wind. Night thick with stars. But look,
What silent tumult in the crash
And roar above, where pincers of the flailing Crab
Rip the void, and Scorpion whirls its sting,
Red giant swells and supernovae glare
To smash the sullen dwarf and fling
Themselves into annihilation,
And mad Dog slavers at the mauling Bear.

Brushing between high banks I trail
The terrier that threads the dark ahead
And holds in grizzled age his proper ground
Snuffling in the ditch, startling
A bird from sleep, beasts coughing in a byre—
Bird, beasts, dog, man, mere

Specks of carbon capering
(Not at will) in figure of the dance,
The mad molecular quadrille
That weaves through wind and water, earth and fire,
The reel and shock of time and chance.

III

What rock split our keel, pitched us
On this cold melancholy shore
With sea-wrack, star-fish, fossils
Powdering underfoot? We salvage
What we can, comb
The beach for driftwood, out of sticks,
Stones, bits of tackle build
A makeshift shelter, call it home.

But nothing holds, or will, upon this coast
Where thin ghosts of the famished poor
Keen like gulls about the headlands still.
Here blade strikes rock, no soil is turned to tilth.
Here Norman, Saxon, figures in a mist
Loomed briefly large before
They too were sucked into the bog;
And here the stricken galleons rolled
Under, spewing corpses, blood, silk, vomit, gold.

Grey shawls pulled round their heads,
The mountains squat beside the sea
Like ancient paupers, vapid eyes
Outstaring still their sum of miseries.

IV

Some came to fast and pray—bent knees
Drilling the cell's cold, dark, gaze
Fixed on God to earth the flash
Of lightning that would shiver them to ash,
Such fearful consummation. After
That sudden sharp distress
What languor, emptiness
Which only the gull's cry fills with long lament
Dissolving into silence as the days
Melt like footprints in wet sand.

The bones earth ground in granite teeth,
Wind honed, wave whitened on this shore
Or fire consumed, may fire beyond
The temporal convulsive stars
(Gone cold at last) at last restore.

WASTE
for Sam Ross

Is what goes down the plug-hole of our lives:
Not just the body's scum, or overplus
Of those combustible materials the gut
Ingests and voids; not simply rags and bones,
Old bedsteads, boots—the clutter that surrounds
All human habitation. Use the world
As sewer or sump, and something yet survives.
It is not even idleness, a foolish tune
Jigging round the head, but accidie,
That medieval sin which middle-age,
Still cumbered by the other fatal six,
Flounders into. In my youth it was no more
Than a cesspool I could jump with ease.
But what is this monstrous slag-heap at the door,
Sprouting weeds and willowherb, fumes
Seeping from its sides, its foul
Bulk breathing into my shut rooms?

PROPER NAMES

Ballydehob, for instance,
Couldn't be anywhere else
Or other than Ballydehob;
Or Skibbereen name anything

But Skibbereen. A few
Lack quiddity. Almost any map
Will find you Michelstown and yet
The word wants suchness of the man

Or place. Some deceive. Thus
Magheramorne bells Comgall's birth,
Ends as lunar crater, deep in dust.
Mullingar grinds souls, its Cross a flail,

Church a ponderous dark mill
Pulverising men. What rough crook there
For Patrick's strays? In croak
Of pomp, that bull-frog's grin, what solace?

But Dingle, Bantry, Baltimore—
Old traffickers by south and west
Salt-blistered—lure with sea-mew's cry: sprawl
In lethargy, their timbers sprung,

Their tackle strewn, like Spanish sail
Storm-spent, among the pitching stars
And welter of the firmament
Foundering in swart Atlantic night.

PROBLEM FAMILY

Squalling brats
They get under my feet all day,
Tugging my sleeve, scuffling with each other
For attention, dribbling
At mouth and nose. I cuff
And curse but can't disown them, too
Like me, warts and all.

That they should sing
Like nightingales is not to be expected
Then. Maybe one day they might learn
To fend for themselves
And master the sparrows' knack
Of vanishing at will into the hedgerows
With a derisive wink of the tail.

RECLUSE

Years ago you slammed your door
And banged the shutters too
On prowlers, strays, the luckless and the lost.
Now, the bolts are all so rusted in
Nothing, nobody can get through,
Not even to interrogate your ghost.

PLACE AND TIME

Climbing the stair this scowling night
I think of all the private clutter now
In curtained rooms—underclothing
Strewn on chairs, pills and bottles, specs and teeth,
The rumpled sheets, the coupling and the snorting—
And all the jabbering tongues of Europe
Sinking slowly into silence, one by one.

Outside, the North Atlantic gnaws
And slobbers on occluded cliffs.
A continent away Aegean islands
Glitter in the light of Sappho's moon
Like jewels on a scented throat. Between,
Millions adrift, castaways
Alone on an illimitable sea

Who will stir beneath the unheard thunder
Of tomorrow's sun, reassuming selves
And clothes which mask the small indignities
Of flesh. I reach out with a stiffening hand
To dowse the light, and turn onto my side—
You changeless as a snapshot in my mind,
Nausicaa turning on the strand

That cerule morning, when her handmaids fled,
To greet the stranger hosted by his dead.

BACK WATER

Tranquil in the sun, the suburbs drowse
Among their flower-beds and lawns. Here tea
Is taken at the customary hour
And chiming clocks in velvet-curtained rooms
Set time in order still: day by day
Signal small imperatives to those
Who pay their taxes and observe the law
Though the Goths loll in the Senate, though
Their once chaste daughters open eager thighs
To the slouching, gun-hung mercenaries.

ALL FOR HECUBA

My forte was the small supporting rôle
In genteel comedy: as the choleric Uncle, say,
Home from the East to find the old place changed,
Or the owl-like Vicar hooting with dismay
At the nice girl's tiff with her nice fiancé
On the eve of the wedding.

Why then do I ham
Through this lugubrious provincial tour
Jeered by drunks, a disaffected populace—
The text corrupt, the props in pawn, no pay
From a bilking management at home—
And there, beyond the foul-mouthed market-place,
A castle with the look of Elsinore?

NEKUIA

Those landfalls on the coasts of death. Twice
That sudden wind, rumble of darkened earth,
Then silence, torches, shades
Crowding the reeded mudbanks and the splash
Of oars through fog. And then to be hauled
Bewildered back into the light, twice
Wrested from the tri-form goddess's sway.
Did Orpheus turn in longing
Or despair, to see his once fleet love
Dragging reluctant limbs towards the day?

NIGHT-FERRY

Winking headlands dowsed by dawn
Smudge to shore on either bow. The Lough
Wrinkles, swells, a slow fat slug
Mounting Belfast's languid loin

Slobbing rocks from which gulls rise
To drift astern. Like rusty tramps
Mills and wharves slide broadside on,
Dribbling slops from their stained sides.

Confetti strews the puddled quay
Where wedding-parties roared farewell
The night before or sobbed through veils
To watch the stern-lights fade. Beyond

Wall-slogans run like wet mascara
Down gable-ends. The terraces
Wear jilted looks, deserted
In the morning, swollen-eyed,

But last night's rain has rinsed the streets
Of last night's vomit, last night's blood.
'Where to, sir?' asks the taximan. 'Home,'
I say. 'Where's that?' 'Home's here,' I say, 'for good.'

TERMINUS

This bedlam in my head, like Waterloo
At rush-hour on a winter afternoon—
The headlines shouting their vacuity,
Rain rattling the roof, wind gusting
Under the portico, whirling scraps about,
Fug in the bars and faces belched
In spasms from the Tube, and feet
Trampling causeways through the straw and mud
While out of darkness into the dark
Trains arrive at random or depart—
I would put it all in order if I could
Muster the will. But intermittent voices
In the eaves (those muffled messages)
Deceive me still with hope
That the chaos might yet be fruitful:
That lovers meeting underneath the clock,
No matter how bedraggled, travel-stained,
Will waken at a touch to innocence
In flowering Eden.

REMEMBRANCE OF THINGS PAST

'Fortunatus et ille, deos qui novit agrestis.'

The rural gods? Those rough bucolics rich
In recollection of stored barns
And cattle steaming in the byre? No.
Among the clattering mills my pals
At Coal Clough Elementary School
Clumped about in their elder brothers' clogs
And their fathers' trousers cut off at the knee
With baggy backsides. In winter when the wind
Mottled bare ribs beneath their tattered jerseys,
Their noses dribbled snot; and sour
As the urinal in the yard the smell
Of fifty to a class, packed tight for warmth.

Forgive me then, whose song is from that sump
Of raucous poverty. Better thus to caw
Than cackle with the disapproving geese
Because their sons at universities
Turn scruffy now by choice.

A STUDY IN SEPIA

Slender as swans they drift back into view,
The High School Fifth, fluttering from chrysalis
Of gym-slip and silk blouse that summer term
About their mistress in a floral dress.

And here's the Sixth Form at the Grammar School
In flannels loitering, the lucky few—
Captains of this or that, text-books under arm—
With brains or parents well enough to do.

No future in its gaze the hungry town
Trudged on the tether of the dole, head down,
Unshaven, collarless, past silent sheds

Sprouting dock and nettle. And barely nods,
Jaw clamped tight still, to see the migrants come,
Stragglers from a beaten army, limping home.

SOUTH MANCHESTER REVISITED

These sooty, tree-lined terraces
Are melancholy as the last of cricket
At summer's end: long afterglow
Of the opulent Victorian sunset

Memory a dry leaf
Powdering underfoot.

PERIPETEIA

In the age before school-milk and meals
His mother came to feed him every day
At mid-morning break, passing buns
And biscuits through the railings. Still pale
And thin and woebegone, he took
His nickname with him to the grammar-school.
'Pansy,' we yelled. He stuck it doggedly
Until he left to take a humdrum job
As a clerk in some insurance office.
Came the war. Pansy swept off all the prizes.
When I saw him last he was sporting a pipe
And a smashing girl and wings and medal-ribbons
And gold-leaf on his cap. 'Er. . . hello,' I said,
By this conjunction of sudden Mars
And Venus thoroughly discomfited
And trying to avoid his soubriquet.
He waved and passed on. He had forgotten me,
No doubt, subfusc in civvies anyway.

CORNCRAKE IN OCTOBER

All summer long through my lank youth
I mooned round this town's edge—corncrake concealed
Among the tufts, connoisseur of disused pits,
Choked culverts, slag-heaps, cuts,
Old cars slumped on their axles in the ditch.

Now, I scale the stumpy streets and pause
To catch my breath on terraces like chopped
Logs smouldering on the charred hillside,

Then crunch across a cinderpad, trampling
Nettles and tall willowherb aside

To gain my one-time habitat
And turn. Out of the smudging rain and blur
Of time, you dart into my mind
Like the flash of a kingfisher's wing
Skimming the stunted lives and dereliction

Almost forty years ago. Rare visitor
With moulted plumes and bristles on my chin
I stumble through the tufted grass as day
Ebbs and down the reach of memory, a swan
Asleep, you drift into the dusk away.

DALESMEN IN CRAVEN

Like lovers they run
Their fingers down your knuckled spine
And long cool flanks. It is they will age
Plodding against the pull

Of gravid earth, breasting the rise
To wrestle your storms or keep
Blue days on bleating fells: who know
Your clints and grykes, each stony mood

And many voices murmuring
From beck and force. But to them
You are young forever, comely
In your green and white. Gruff fire

Of Norseman, Saxon, Dane
Glints through their gutturals
Like igneous rock, grudged speech
Venting the stubborn rage within

To have and hold snug thwaite,
The clinking farms where sheep-dogs bark
By sett or side. Dent and Hawes
And Hubberholme—the names

Tongue stopped mouths still like tenor bells
Booming in the dales, Nordic base
That grounds your passion of Celtic song
From Penyghent, your intricate

Descants and riddling
Falls through chambered stone. Blent,
Wild blood and slow move in measure, mount
As anthem, polyphonic, eloquent.

HURSTWOOD

Edmund Spenser lived here once in youth, head full
Of pastoral hexameters and Chaucer,
By holm and sheepfold, beck and force
Shaping the grunting North's grudged gutturals
Into mellifluous speech—Kilcolman yet
Unthought of and the last
Headlong flight that shattered all the dream.
The stead still stands, the hamlet hardly changed,
A dark dent in the moors. Rough-blocked stone
Tumbles about its crooked street
At knock-kneed angles where beasts steam
In byres, and cow-pats plump around your feet.

Beyond, firmly at the first drystone walls,
Marching uphill, enfold the stubborn farms,
Then falter, straggle, splay
Among the tussocks, fall at last
Where sheep-tracks fail. Dunting the north,
Bull-necked, backs shoved against the skyline,
Extwistle and Boulsworth guard their own,
That fastness of wild weather lurking there
Malignant still though men forget,
Unmindful in their cities. And Widdop crowds
The east, black muster of bald crag, bent thorn,
Reeded pool which rain-scud pimples then beclouds.

Always it lay there, humped across my childhood,
That mute, swart mass, by merry aunts
Unexorcised or big voiced, boisterous men
Out carolling on Christmas Eve,
Or thrill of games each Boxing Day

About the ice-cold corridors and raftered rooms
In darkness or by candlelight. Those gay
Girls gone, the big men downed
Who bent their brawn against its bulk.

And shifting malice, how they sag
And chunner in the wind, old barn
Old farmstead now. The chopped
Cold clang across the fields
Of Worsthorne's church-bell beats old bones
Beneath the slabs, chaws
Time in iron teeth, its bitten note
Leaving no echo in the air. I drag

That bleakness deep within me: though
Sometimes in summer briefly, briefly
Over the brow of silence sings the lark.

NOT IN THE BROCHURE

By plane this time, by coach they come,
Relentless as the horsemen of Attila,
Swarming south to cluster on the coast
Where, methodically taking off their clothes,
They settle to the serious business
Of acquiring a suntan. This done, some stare
At the ruined monuments: but mostly
The young make love while the old (Artemis
Brauronia, in these thyme-scented hills)
Bother about their bowels and hope in vain
That you may yet incline yourself towards them
And grant them potency.

NO SECOND TROY?

Well past (for the most part) military age,
We clamber stiffly from the coach. A wind
Kicks dust into our eyes. That detail, then,
At least is true. And indeed the terrain
In general corroborates the ground-reports
Filed by an earlier party—the sea,
The coastal plain and, on this ridge, the citadel.

I think of the choleric incompetents
Blustering in high command, fudging the blame
For failures; the beefy, insolent louts,
Flouting discipline, bedding their boys
Or women; and the bitten ranks, year after year
Squelching through the butchery and boredom.
It has happened often enough, this slow

Exsanguination by siege, though rarely
Has the pursuit of the final solution
Demanded such persistence. Yet men crept back,
Rebuilding. In Roman times the city
Achieved both spaciousness and opulence. It lost
Utility at last not through catastrophe
But (I should guess) a shift of the trade routes

Which left it high and dry, though not forgotten—
As witness us, camp-followers arrived
Millennia too late, rummaging the site
To find the show is over, the pickings few:
That two queer buffers long since dead
(One old and blind, the other of middle years
And a valetudinarian)

Who neither of them ever even visited
The place, cornered the glory, and the tears.

APOCALYPSE

Legend says they were let down
On golden chains from heaven, these shrines
Whose icons glimmer faintly
In the gloom—replicas on earth

Of sacred polity. To us,
The boreal white-faced
Barbarians, traipsing after guides
And gods resplendent in the risen light,

Such mysteries seem cramped and dark.
Yet this cave here beside the path
Is and was from the beginning. We stoop
Beneath the rock and stumble round

In silence, half-blinded still. A monk
Hands me a tract I cannot read
Or even thank him for. I fidget
By his massive dignity

And notice that you too have stood
Apart—one of the olive-skinned
Unfathomably dark-eyed Greeks—
While all the rest disperse. You drop

A coin into the empty box, light
And place a candle, pause
A moment, staring up, then turn
Quickly away, brushing through cascades

Of scarlet blossom brilliant
Against white stone. I follow,
Wordless, though the tongue
Stammers in my head—with what cry stung

Of hidden grief: what spurt of song?

DOLPHINS

According to Aesop they were witty
As well as amiable: bland
In back-chat with lions or apes. Poets
They instantly befriended, in shipwreck
Or calamity offering a broad back
And a fast run to a neighbouring island
Or any neutral port. Yet they were not,
Ever, to be trifled with. Suddenly today
They flywheel alongside or spin like black
Projectiles past the stern. But from what
Depths, through what green silences they come,
Exulting in their elemental joy,
Who knows? And who can fathom
Why they swerve, hallooing down our wash away?

THE LAST ALEXANDRIAN

I rummage through his multiple disguises
Searching for the essence of the man—
This Greek turned Englishman turned Greek again,
Clerk who trudged for thirty years by day
In the Third Circle of the Irrigation Office
With starched high collar, sober suit, pince-nez
And carefully protruding cuffs: cautious, mean,
Cutting his cigarettes in half: then
Pursuing his outrageous lusts by night
In furtive alleys: true Hellene
Memorializing all that dross,
The lassitude and squalor and evasion
And fallen splendours fused in verse
Shot through with glory like an iron,
Sombre, elegiac, serene.

SCHERIA

What visions in that leaping light,
Odysseus? What wonders in the deep?

Ten years of Troy humped on your back,
Bunched in the stern you ran (you said)
For home. Was it simply for the tale's sake, then,
Or on some impulse that you sheered
So wide, all sea-marks sunk beneath
The known horizon? Your lads could count the odds
You faced: the winds perverse, the gods
Malevolent. Dead reckoning, they knew,
Was not your way. But trafficking
With monsters, under the world's rim
Raising ghost—this was madness which your crew

Every man-jack, paid for in the end.
By then, not Circe's wand
Or any song Calypso sang
Could give you back your human shape,
Sea-monster flopped ashore
And gasping in your blubber on the strand:
Only

That slim girl like a slender palm
Growing on Delos who, smiling, took you by the hand.

SCHOLAR EMERITUS

As Lesbos rose on the port bow
He perched high on the gangway, perilously
Clutching his book and waving a megaphone,
And read to the sunbathers sprawled below—
His dry voice rasping like the amplified
Recording of a cricket—Sappho
On the symptoms of immoderate desire.
'When I look on you, suddenly my tongue
Fails me. Delicate fire runs through my flesh.
My eyes swim. I sweat. I tremble ...' Then,
Picking up his stick, he limped away
And left them to their sleep.

II
                              In Ragusa,
Later, hot and querulous his wife
Stopped me in the street. 'Where has he got to now?
What does he mean, leaving me here like this
Without a dinar for these cards?' I paid
While she protested still. But he was only
Leaning on a parapet above the walls
Nearby, and blinking mildly out to sea—
Regretting, perhaps, the nightingales and roses,
But much more likely (for I too was puffed
By the climb) reflecting that short breath
And singing ears, a pounding heart, can have
An aetiology distinct, alas, from love.

THASOS

Morning sparkles in the bay
Like sapphire in a clasp of pearl. Boats
Chuckle now ashore. This
Island in antiquity
Thrived on gold from Thrace and wine
Famous for its excellent bouquet.

We climb a steep hillside through the woods,
Pausing on the summit by a shrine
Sacred once to Pan. I puff
Like an old walrus, grateful for the rest

And view. There must be dolphins far below
Cartwheeling round these coasts in zest.

But it is time to go,
You say, unbreathed, sure-
Footed as a faun, and lead
Down a vertiginous descent
Beside the tumbled blocks of stone
Where some old craftsman notched his signature

In perpetuity. Thence,
Past children, olive-brown, who stare
With eyes like oysters at the strangers,
We came back once more to the square
Beside the harbour where we stop for drinks.
And that is all, except that I

Am drunk already, having no need
Of wine; and know now why
That simple man, Archilochus,
Refused, and pitched his shield into the bush.

ITHACA

Beyond the black, rumbustious straits
Blurred harbour-lights heave into view.
I lurch onto the deck. A raw
Nor'easter rams the splintered landing-stage
Where figures flit in shadow, crouch
To grab our hawsers, winch us home.

Home? Is this then truly Ithaca
Again? The idiom ashore
Tastes salt-familiar yet strange, cuts
Like whipcord. Cloud-scurry and that one bleak star
Above the cliff-line massing north
Confirm a low meridian. What gifts

Have I or any brought this stony land,
Save empty hands, a few tall tales? They say
The roads this night are red with fire and blood.
But who are the usurpers? Who divides
Our patrimony? And when the dawn-mist lifts,
Which beggar shall be recognised as king?

A WINTER JOURNEY

I

Twenty-five years ago I hiccuped sobs
And snivelled through my father's funeral.
Pale in black beside me you were mute
As in a dream—no gesture but the sudden
Fierce white grip of your hand on mine
When the coffin slowly passed from sight
For ever.

      Afterwards Old Uncle Frank—
Falstaff to my youth, white-haired
And limping on his stick—drew me aside,
'This is no way, you whining cub,
To help your mother.' But I had done
With tears by then. Your agony,
Crushing my hand, had wrung me dry.

II

How cold the grieving house. That night
All starving Europe to the Urals froze,
Glinting under ice. We huddled
Round the grate, trying to warm numbed flesh,
Numbed minds to life. But even the quick
That winter, sixth and worst of war,
Seemed shrunken as the sheeted dead
Or sunk in catatonic trance—jerked
At last from stupor by the shock
And murderous spasm of the Spring.

III

Now, from windy Ireland struggling home
Through lashed airports, black turbulence of cloud—
Shap blocked, the roads a quagmire—I have come
Too late. Ice fumes the windows of the room
In which you lie, your frail flag struck, the siege
Slow-mounting, ended in this brutal sack.
The crusted pomps—how soon—and blazonry
Of that cold triumph deck you, sealed
In stiff heraldic silence: seize this house

Which gathers its flesh to grieve
In whispers, dying without issue. What rock
Shall found our hope, except hushed earth,
This shrunken season while we mourn your wrack,
Hides under straw dark huddle of a birth?

IV

How many times have I come home
With my small trophies like a dog
To lay them at your feet, nuzzling
Your hand for approbation?

What have I brought you now, so shrunk
By death I cannot bear
To look on you in that cold room
Or other to look? A pair

Of gold-rimmed specs (my first
In middle-age) to make
You laugh: the jacket of a book
(My only child, late born) which I

Had named for you, that you might die
Knowing something fathered for your sake.

V

Seeing you were the last of all
Your long-lived generation, nieces
Nephews came in force—once gay
Once boisterous—to the funeral,
Stamping feet, complaining of the cold
In boots and furs, most in their sober
Sixties now, some deaf, some lame, all grey.

Knelt, broke their fast with us, have gone
Wedged in cars with promises
To meet somewhere sometime again.
I turned back to the house alone,
Finding all dark and silent. But when
I flung the curtains open, every room
Filled with such light no wintry sun

Could give, so gentle, so benign,
It seemed this day had never come.

VI

Above my lumbering turbo-prop a jet
Arrows out to the Atlantic, white
Feathers of its vapour-trail outspread,
Streaming towards the sunset. I watch
It plunge into the bull's-eye while we tread
Cloud like tundra lumped below, lurch
Through chasms, drifts, nosing now—flaps down—
For Ireland. So, the fixed star gone
Of my triangulated life, I grope
Towards my landfall. May I home
Still through all weathers; come
Into the circle of remembered light
Which strips all false anatomies, the sleight

Of summer, spring's deceit: from loss, from hurt
Composing a true landscape of the heart.

RUNNING REPAIRS
(1983)

You will not find other places, other seas.
This city will follow you. Through the same streets,
The same neighbourhoods, you will wander and grow old.
—C.P. Cavafy, 'The City'

THEOLOGIAN

Stooped, blinking at the light, he shambled in,
Lifted up his head, lifted massive paws,
And with hardly a glance at his notes discoursed
For an hour or more. And surely I thought
His mouth was smeared with honey and his huge
Arms crushed the hushed hall to his breast
In clumsy tenderness. But next to me
A young girl screwed her mouth into a yawn,
Fingered her bracelet, raised a hand to smooth
Her cascade of bright hair. In blood's blind jig,
The dream of flesh engrossed, why should she
With this gaunt old man hunger for discarnate truth?

SPIRIT OF PLACE

These days I know you only
By your absences, the landscape
Empty and inert: or when,
Still nowhere to be seen, you nonetheless

Look coldly on me, intruder
On your lonely dance at noon,
Transgressor of your woods and streams,
Your pastures and your drumlins.

It was not always so. Once,
Furze crowned the rounded hills,
Gold chaplets of your bravery;
Your banks hid snowdrop, primrose,

Violet. I dipped my hands
Into the rills, and felt your touch
Like cool silk on me: all your weathers
Running through my flesh like fire.

COLUMKILLE

I

The mountains sprang to guard his birth,
Bald sentinels, their molten wars
Transfixed for ever in arrest of rock;

Or wheeling at full gallop froze,
White manes flying in the wind,
To flank him from the sea. For him

Salmon crammed the sound by night
Between Horn Head and Tory
To flail upstream and thud at dawn

About his feet. Beside his stead
The blackbird sang on spangled thorn
And honeysuckle in the hedges

Twined with pale dog-rose to weave
Him coronets of sleep. Among
The shadows of God's plentitude

The eagle soared. What hurled him then
Headlong, the great breasted storm, his pinions
Scattered in the eye of risen sun?

II

Now, nothing's left but legends and a few
Stones standing in the windy west. Year by year
I come to track him and interrogate
The sole remaining witness—a bony hag
Tricked in a torn green skirt. Too many ghosts
Ramble among her memories. She dreams
Of youth and an imagined rape
Committed on once lovely limbs, of wild geese
Swallowed in the storm, of ships
With human cargo starving in their holds
Among the rats and cholera. I piece
The tale together. Some of it makes sense.
The rest is maundering, not evidence.

Suppose her foul mouth, though, and riddling tongue
Speak oracles? Suppose that tripod stool,
The spittle drooling from her lips, her knotted hair
And staring eyes are mantic? My lot came
To plant and build and to possess, sweeping
Down from Derry, pragmatic in their phlegm:
But could not read the omens then
And will not now. The English vice, it seems,
Is not hypocrisy but cosiness,
A bland refusal to admit extremes
Whether of evil or of holiness—
As if good manners, charm and chintz
Could tame the tiger at the gate or win
To household tricks the beast within.

III

What shimmers through the golden haze?
No dove, an eagle towering in the sun,
That gaunt figure with the staff
And beaked, square head and burning eyes
Advancing with the symbols of his wrath.

I stare again. Shadows reel
Across the bog. On flat-backed Muckish cloud-scud
Skims, and darkens. White-pointed Errigal
Bursts the sodden bag of rain, and all
Vistas vanish as the land

Runs westward with its decks awash
Pitching into winter. We cling to spars
And cordage, drowning in the common night
Of history with that warrior-saint
Engulfed, who stumbled once towards the light.

LENT

East by north all winter through
Wind dropped at last, hoarfrost thick
On bole and bank, the ponds
Glazed over, songbirds silent. Only

The whins fought back, burnished shields
Embushed by the wayside, flaring
In the smouldering red dusk
Of ice-bound days. Then, at winter's end,

This sudden turbulence,
Tormenting the stripped trees'
Arthritic limbs, flattening
Pelt and fur, flings hail, rocks mind

From moorings, scatters me like straw.
They give no ground though, ever,
Barbaric in their splendour
Of Mycenaean gold: beset by thorns

Burst through now to resurrection.

A STATEMENT IS EXPECTED SHORTLY

Thrace devastated now, the barbarians
Are marching, it is rumoured, on the Capital,
Their vanguard raising thunderclouds of dust.
Already, looters fire the suburbs, and carts
Piled high with household goods and children
Jostle through the gates. In the foreign quarter
A disaffected rabble stones the guards,
Screaming abuse. The Emperor is aghast.
He weeps before the Council, whose members
Have dispatched an embassy with gifts
For the barbarian king, and a dignified
Remonstrance in faultless Attic prose
Which hints at subsidy: though the Treasury,
In fact, is empty. They sigh.
There is nothing more to be done. Meanwhile
It is important to keep up appearances.
Perhaps the Empress Mother may be moved
To admonish her son. She at least believes
In the miraculous intervention of the Virgin.

VISITATION

I recognised first the gesture,
Then the voice, and then
The glance of sunlight on your hair
Swept back like a raven's wing. So,
Even before you turned towards me,
My heart knocked in its cage
And I dropped my gaze lest my eyes
Be scorched by your presence.
When I looked up again
You were gone: not to be found
In the weary crowds, shuffling here
Through dust and stones and heat.

PANTECHNICON
for Padraic Fiacc

This thing goes faster and faster. Brakes worn,
Tyres frayed, the steering wobbly and the road
Dropping ahead, the whole contraption
Jolting, rattling, lurching under its load

Is bound to crash soon. But look through the mirror
Behind, and the past moves in slow motion
Like a cricket-match in a sunlit field, or
Stands frozen in mid-gesture, figures on

A marble frieze—the perspectives all foreshortened,
Your friends, your loves still in their prime, smiling
So that you might turn to greet them, mend
The foolish quarrels, threads snapped in the dark labyrinth

Of time: or would if you weren't bucketing downhill,
Scared to death and hanging onto the wheel.

END OF SEASON

Like a playful smack on a barmaid's bottom
The flood tide slaps and fondles the sea-wall
In summer while the world strolls by.

But see what the ebb, this winter afternoon,
Reveals: broken bottles, condoms, cans, the green
Dribble of a rusty sewer.

And only the old are left here now
With gulls for company, red-beaked scavengers
Screaming in the bitter wind.

PROVINCIA DESERTA

Well, here it is: not Botany Bay
But a penal settlement all the same,
The sentence life without remission—saving,
Of course, Sir, such as yourself, gentlemen newly come
To live here at the Governor's Lodge. Two years from now
You will be safely home again and dining out
On your bizarre experiences, which cannot fail
To please your hostess and amuse the company.

Let me then briefly sketch our way of life. First,
Custom binds us, hardly ever law. Mating,
Which takes the mind off other things,
We openly encourage, especially
For procreation: but only, note, within each tribe.
(Exogamy means instant ostracism.)
Condemned at birth, children are consigned
By parents to our priests for prompt initiation
In rituals of wrath, the wind of vengeance.
All punishment is random and condign, each
Adult male doubling as both predator
And victim—a symbiosis which ensures
All suffer in the end alike. Please don't be
Alarmed, though. Well-trained squads clean up the carnage
And maintain tolerably hygienic conditions
For temporary survivors.

                    You find this strange,
No doubt; and stranger still our fierce
Cleaving to the only thing
We share and murder for. It is a land,
You see, of quite surpassing beauty,
Of stream and mountain, lake and wood
With many haunting presences

Which will shadow you always, beckoning
Still, however far your country.

BACK TO THE BASICS

Here we go again: pulse, temperature,
Blood tests, blood-pressure, samples of urine,
X-ray, electrocardiogram. Any
Chest-pain, shortness of the breath? How soon,
Old hands or new, we settle to the strict routine
Of their impersonal compassion.
O yes—and here's the motherly old hen,
Convalescent now, who clucks about the ward
In her dressing-gown, comforting the lonely
Or the shy; who always has a reassuring smile
For anxious visitors at the next bed;
And used to being useful, helps the hard-
Pressed nurses hand out early morning tea.

QUIS MULTA GRACILIS ... ?

Short back-and-sides, I slump into a chair
Vacated by a long-haired youth,
And dodging what the mirror shows me stare
At a slogan on the wall. 'Better For Both',
It says, picturing a tall, bronzed man, coat slung
Across his shoulder, right arm round
His laughing girl, leading her through summer fields
Towards a copse. Shampooed now, back-combed, scent-sprayed,
The young on either side hitch up their jeans
And go, toileted for Aphrodite
Whose wares augment this barber's trade.

I think of the Spartans at Thermopylae
Preening themselves for death. But history
Is silent elsewhere on the way
They coped—no pill, no sheath, visiting their girls
By stealth. Better for both? Who knows? Probably
The same old sorry human mess, I'd say.

SOUTERRAIN

I wonder about this Macedonian
Painted in his pomp, his Asian triumphs
Fresh still in the public mind, by Hermes now
Wafted towards the seat of judgement. Surely
Distinguished service overseas to king
And country should settle matters in his favour
Once for all—the exigencies of war
And, here or there, a little indiscriminate
Slaughter notwithstanding. (A wise general
Must learn to give his troops their head at times.)
Besides, from all he had heard his judges too
Were gentlemen, devoted to blood-sports
In their day, and horses, drink and women.
If not, he could always bully and bawl
At them like raw recruits on his parade-ground
At Pydna long ago.

        But do I detect
A slight unease beneath his arrogance,
A certain faltering of stride? Let me
Salute him then in this windless place,
The sense of failure settling like fog
On both of us, met here beside the path
That winds through reeds and marshland, its cold
Silence chilling the mind, acrid in the mouth.

PILLAR OF SOCIETY

Yes, he hankered for respectability
All right, accumulating honours. But
To his womenfolk at least he must have been
A trial to live with, finicky and glum
Never satisfied with what he'd got,
Fancying himself indeed—at his age
Too, silly old cod—with high-born ladies
And craving fresh infatuation.
And all the while, out of the weed-grown past
And walled-off gardens of his mind in autumn
He plucked his golden fruit. The whole performance
Was ridiculous. But then the muse takes lodging
Where she will: this ancient in his dotage,
That dowdy, ill-used woman in her grave.

CANDLES

I have lit candles for you all through Greece
In censed cool silences, golden gloom
Out of the heat and glare; in dusty shrines
Of disused monasteries foundering
Beneath wistaria and clematis,
The rust-green drag of barnacled decay;
In chapels perilous among the mountains
Where lost Byzantium's faint afterglow

Illumines last hieratic gestures, spells
Against the dark. The mysteries burn within
Of the crucified god, anguish of love,
Of loss. Beyond, spread scents of thyme and tarmarisk,
White townships cascading to waterfronts,
Horizons of the purple-stained Aegean.

JOURNEYS END

Expresses glide now into termini; screws
Threshing astern, ferries inch towards quays;
And whistling jets thump down on runways, roar
Suddenly and trundle to a stop. All void

Their passengers into the city's maw
Where other travellers wait
In lounge-bars or in crowded cafeterias
Among beer-stains, baggage, cigarette stubs, tea

Slopped in saucers, for trains or planes or buses.
Humanity's endemic mess apart,
These migrations mostly serve some end
Of public gain or private profit. A few

Are blessed, in the pale March sun
Bringing together separated lovers
Across great continents or estuaries
To ease them of their ache.

HOW TO BECOME AN ALEXANDRIAN

You lecture in English. This confers prestige
(It is better to lecture than to teach)
And creates a presumption of knowledge.

There are other advantages—short hours,
Long holidays, security of pay
And tenure, a captive audience

Of the impressionable young. What's more,
You can display as much aggression
And look as scruffy as you please

On or off the job. In no time at all
You will be asked to parties, will appear
On platforms to prolonged applause

For your courageous stand against oppression
At home here or abroad. You might—who knows?—
Be seen some off-peak evening on the telly,

Crammed bum and belly into crotch-tight jeans,
By far the hairiest of the panel
Of show-biz tarts and talkative old queans.

HIGHER HODDER

On Hodder Bridge I pause to map
Under its slow white sail of cloud
The full-rigged landscape freighted now
With summer's load. Trout slide,
Slim shadows, into dark green pools
Below. At matins in the grass
Crickets chirr their dry descant
Shrilly on the dale's deep murmur.
My grandfather at eighty fished this stream
Walking the green heart still of grace
On mornings like this morning thick
And drowsy with the musk of may.

Like holm-oaks gripping ground they grew,
Stone by knuckled stone, the gnarled

Arthritic villages—Chipping,
Slaidburn, Whitewell, Downham, Mitton—
Pitched in a pentagram askew
About this spot. Silting slow
In time, their musty churches fly
Crossed banners still against oblivion.
But how can that frail figure stay
The worm within; or bell-tower bind
That counts instead the silent loss, drip
By drip, of the leaking world's life-blood?
Demdike and Chattox in my father's day
Were names to scare a child: witches creaked,
Wild geese across the moon. A stricken
Paradise it must have been
Which luckless generations fled
To fill the rumbling bellies of the mills
Famished for their flesh—snuffed wick
Smouldering by night beyond the hills,
All fire, all freshness poisoned to the quick.

Strange, then, how this broad dale tugs
The mind at farthest reach—through sheer
Salt weather homing, fog, an ice-fanged sea—
To tether it at last. Now
I catch my hands in middle-age
Making my father's gestures, mark them
His hands upon the rough warm stone
At rest, stiffening here while sun
Bursts seed and all the crescent year
Burns to June's core. I grow these days
Downwards, back into the moil
Of masticating earth. Among
Old bones, old boulders, stumps of rotten tree
The blind roots clutch and curl; and ways
Not my ways knurl my trunk, bend, slowly master me.

BUT FOR YOUR GIFTS
from the Greek of Nicephoros Brettakos

But for your gifts, Lord, of poetry
What should I have to live on now?
These fields would not be mine:
Whereas I rejoice here in my apple-trees,

Rejoice that my stones have fructified,
That my cupped palms fill with sunlight,
My desert with people,
My garden with nightingales.
And what do you think of them, Lord? Have you seen
My sheaves of corn? Have you seen my vines?
How pleasant is the light that falls
On my sheltered valleys?

And I still have time.
I have not yet cultivated all my land.
Pain clears my plot, ploughs me deeper still.
I scatter my laughter like shared bread, yet
I do not spend your sun improvidently,
I do not let fall even a crumb of what you give me:
Because I am mindful of the storms of winter,
Of the nightfall soon to come. Before I go
I must make my hut a church
For the shepherds of love.

AFTER THE BOMBING

Between the fire-tongued shells of warehouses
And boarded-up shop windows, hand in hand,
They came hurrying down the street, laughing
Together and smiling at each other,
Then paused at the kerb to snatch a kiss
Before stepping across the road still strewn with glass
And vanishing down an alleyway—so
Blithe, so radiantly swift
Their passage that it swung the mind away,
The needle oscillating those few seconds
From hate's dead reckoning.

TRAVELLING WESTWARD

Travelling westward this day through the shires,
Worcestershire, Gloucestershire and Somerset,
Timbered, cricketing counties tinged with leaf
And blossom in the first faint flush, the stir

Of summer's deep, slow music, I think
Of that farther island in the west,

Her famished fields, whins lighting the loanings,
Stony acres slashed with seams of gold.

I should have left her long since, settled here
Where I belong. Not now. What should I do
Without her, soft-tongued, virginal-seeming
Slut that she is? I have grown old

In her toils, her meltings and evasions,
The narrow quarrel of our fruitless bed.

AT SAUL

Rouse me, March, from this long torpor
Now daffodils at muster blow
Their bugles in the dells and whins
Break cover in the gullies, roar
Up bank and boreen, fire drumlins,
Set byres ablaze, with ragged rush
Of spike and banners swarm below
To storm townlands where shrubs in ambush

Shell-burst, showering gold. Then shake
Me, March, out of my lethargy.
With shrill of wind in wire, earth's strum
And stress, your prologue mounts. Soon thunder-crack
Of riven rock shall split the tomb
And wild sap shoot in the dead Tree.

SCHOLAR IN THE LIBRARY

A flash of legs and high heels past his desk
Diverts his ageing eye (discreet perfume, neat
Blouse and skirt, a trim hair-do), lust's surge
And sudden sharp constriction gripping groin
And throat. Sensing this, she turns and smiles,
Frailer, older, sadder than she had seemed
At first from the rear view. What now? Should Bacchus
Leap upon astonished Ariadne, or
Subside behind his books to hide his shame?

TRIVIA

Crowning these hills, a knot of roads
Drawn tight, unsignposted, snaking here
Through hedgerows: glimpses of sea,
Dark headlands dwindling down the coast;
A shining lough, and mountains
Criss-crossed, netted by the morning sun;
A carious city muttering below
Under the smoke-haze. I halt
Among my contradictions
Warming myself meanwhile against the blaze
Of fuchsias this autumn day. Deeper
Than doubt, more ancient than my tongue can name,
There are powers here hobbling choice. Which way to turn?

SECOND-HAND BOOKSTALL

In the photograph that forms the frontispiece
He stands by Priam's wall, screwing up his eyes
Against the sun, a smiling, slightly built
Young man, not unlike the former Prince of Wales
Travelling in those days incognito
In baggy shorts that reached down to his knees.
The date: April 20th, 1939.

Leafing through his verses now, I see that they
Were dedicated to the King (no less)
Of the Hellenes, their preface by a Head of House
At Oxford—distinguished auspices indeed.
Yet his book, alas, was still-born, filled
Only with nostalgia for the ancient world
But void of suffering or sense of loss.

And anyway, what sort of fist would he
Have made of Troy, I wonder, among the flies
And stink and sweat, the muscle-bound, vainglorious
Louts, the sodomy and rape and slaughter?
In the library at Alexandria now
He might have sat at ease among his kind.
But with scowling Achilles and all that gang?

Still, I shall keep the book. Not by design
But inadvertence it reveals another world
Gone under—of strolling parasols
And blazers through the leisured afternoon
Loitering by river-banks, and croquet
On the lawn, and hand-bells tinkling for tea:
Of England's late Edwardian dream

The final flowering.

TO AN ENGLISH LIBERAL, TEN YEARS ON

They bomb and burn and slaughter still. 'Why yet?' you cry.
The Saxon raped their Mother-goddess.
They want revenge. To hell with your redress.
How else now can they prove their potency?

ENCOUNTERS

Some are by fate, not accident.
You know them not by reckoning the odds
Against coincidence of time and place.
(The statistics of probability
Will teach you nothing.) You know them by
Your shaking heart, the shock of recognition
And shiver in the presence of the numinous.
They are exalting but terrible. And one
May be enough to haunt a lifetime.

IN MEMORIAM G.B. NEWE
from Clinical notes, 1972
'leti discrimina parva'

I

A staff nurse through the sleeping ward
Rustles like a sigh. Tonight my mind
Runs calm and clear: runs all on you,
Old friend, lonely in your distant glen
And vilified by your own kind.
What comfort can I give you then?

I picture you, beside a great turf fire
Reading late or dozing in your chair
While the North Atlantic gasps outside
And gripes through its black gullet from Kintyre
To Benmore Head.

                You knew the cost
Of not stampeding with the rest
Or hurling a bomb or abuse
Was ostracism at the best—
At worst, a bullet in the back.
But 'Charity comes first,' you said,
'Not justice. Justice without charity
Will never reconcile or make us whole.'

Well, those words were mouthed into the gale
And torn away. Against such odds
As faced you for a lifetime none
But a fool would so persist, or one of God's
Own saints—only to see the politics
Of outrage and atrocity prevail.

I've no comfort, then, for you,
Only reasons for despair. Besides,
What's left for you or me to do—
So brittle are the fictions now
That shield us from death's truth—except
To write our memoirs while we may?
'My God, no. Not yet,' you'll say.
'For after charity come faith and hope,
Not self-justification. And anyway,
I've no choice. The work goes on because it must,
And will, long after I am dust.'

I'm not so sure; and yet it comforts me
This pitching night flecked by the spume
And slobber of the maniacal sea
To know the candle shines still in your room.

II
Cushendall, 1982

Ten years ago I wrote that verse
But neither named or sent it to you then.

(The times were out of joint and both of us,
For different reasons, on the danger-list,
Though both of us survived.) Now,
Your throaty chuckle stopped and sideways smile,
You have gone into the world of silence
And I am here this sharp November day—
The sea dead-calm, cold sunlight on the headlands—
To pay my last respects beside your grave.

This was your place, and these your people
Who welcome me, a stranger to their rite,
With rough warm handshakes bonding common grief.
The life you shared with them of cult and creed,
Throb and pulse-beat of the hidden force,
Far older even than your faith, which stirs
In rock, in spring, woodlands of the streaming glen,
I could not touch or share. I knew you
Only as you moved about the world
Beyond these hills, a quiet man
Whose quiet courage and humility
Moved mountains in your time, left fallen humankind
Astonished by its own propensity
For good.

        Never again, this next spring or the next,
Will you see the glens blaze out in glory.
The flame you lit—scholar, mercy's agent
And historian, at rest in your own earth—
Gutters in the wind, your shielding hands
For ever now withdrawn. Swinging here
From doubt to hope, from hope to doubt again,
I turn away, into the rising gale,
Storm-clouds scudding on the peaks, the lash of rain.

AGE

Is the dead patch of the skin that pricked
Yields no sensation

The dry cells of the brain where memory
Has withered at the root

The slag and clinker of a heart gone cold
As body shrinks

Into the posture of the womb again,
Craving warmth.

But most it is the rage
Within of folly and desire, impotence

A hunger-striker
Rattling in vain its gaunt contracting cage.

DIPLOMATIC RECEPTION

Drinks in hand they bellow
At each other through the smoke
Like rival ruby packs confused
About their code. The sheer

Bulk and hairy mass
Of their sweating masculinity
Tramples me under in the ruck. I vanish,
A Cheshire cat behind my smile

Watching them kick and bite and claw
And scramble for advantage. But suppose
I stumbled some night into your chamber,
Queen, a scullion with sullied shift

And greasy brow. Would you too
Ignore me, nullity
Who even in your private presence,
Crouched at your knee, is never seen?

SHIPWRECKED MARINER

That sea-cleft, shadowed coast drew him unaware
Of sudden darkness, storm and reef. Pitched ashore,
He staggered to the clearing where—
Its fragrant wood-smoke drifting though the trees—
Her palace lay. And there for sure she paced
The terrace in the evening light, her hair
Unbound, her handmaids all dismissed,
As if expecting some Odysseus.
What then to do—spring forward, clasp her knees

Mastering her spell? No. To mingle with the goddess
Was not, he knew, for such as him. Must lie
That night and every night
Among the acorns with the grunting swine,
Lost companions in the witch's sty.

SPECIMEN

Where has it gone, that gift
In childhood and youth of concentration
Which nothing almost could disturb? I would fall
Into contemplation like a saint
In a trance: but of things profane—
Some toy or book, a game or a girl—while,
Beyond, the dingy town trudged by in drizzling rain.

Now, when I should fix my thoughts
On my end, repenting all I have done
And not done, repairing what I can, my mind
Wanders, a butterfly by every breeze
Wafted from shrub to flower, from flower to stone
In the sun staggering for scent or warmth. Then
I am gone again, for some fresh chapel of ease

Or wayside shrine at random.
Bees gather honey for the hive, but I
Only brush my world, each passing moment
Mourning the past, with nothing won,
No store, no foothold. Transfix me, then, content
To loiter thus through summer: who from
My chrysalis failed somehow to emerge as man.

DAYBREAK

As, in a silent town, life stirs
Before the dawn, and lights flick on
In curtained rooms at random, so

Wakening, I tiptoe round
Your sleeping form and lift the blind
On empty streets. Like dew

RUNNING REPAIRS

'It won't be much of a job, you understand—
Simply a makeshift minor op.
Under local anaesthetic. Certainly
Things won't be any worse, and given luck
They should be better. A proper job, of course,
Would not only take much longer but
Would call for general anaesthesia
Which is not recommended in your case.'

Not recommended in my case ...? H'm, old
Bangers can't be choosers, I suppose.
And anyway it isn't far from here
To the knacker's yard. 'Oh, very well, then: just
So long as you can keep me on the road.'

MORALITIES

I

Given that human nature gravitates
Always towards the worst, what is to be done?

Strangle the instinctual man, he may
Turn briefly blue but won't stop kicking.

Age brings no cure. It banks the fires;
Craves, more than youth, a bestial ecstacy

Though that is not the worst. Lust at least
Implies relationship, which sometimes

(God knows how) may flower into love.

II

First, merely a donkey's distant bray, the harsh
Honk of the quotidian disturbing

The murmur of an August afternoon
And adolescence dreaming in the sun

Then, with middle age, mephitic, slovenly
Familiar, appropriating bed and board,

Failure settles down to a life-tenancy,
Squats there grosser by the day, to jeer

At body's decay, while outside on the sands
Of summer the young display triumphant flesh

To mark mind's slow, insistent drip, its concentration
Leaking like a tap, to pick the sore

Of being passed over, leap-frogged
By lesser men, or worse, by better

The opportunities foregone for ever,
The blunders all now irretrievable

And love betrayed. For stealing fire
From heaven, vultures tore Prometheus

On the far Caucasian rock. Remorse,
The too-late dawning of self-knowledge

Hanged Judas.

III

God's dead, they say. Old Nobodaddy's done for,
Gone for good, an unnecessary hypothesis—

And therefore not susceptible to proof
One way or the other. But what's for sure

Is that the deadly old gang keep
Their sevenfold cunning, briskly work the crowd

Like tipsters, con-men, tarts on Derby Day,
Their pickings rich as ever: with nudge and wink

Fuel ancient fantasies of flesh
And power, or feed anxiety. Yet

After the fun, what's left behind among
The beer-cans, bottles, bits of paper

Which damp gusts strew on trampled grass,
Is a litter of disappointed hopes,

And odour like the faint, stale
Smell of smegma under the prepuce.

IV

The worst
Is to be humped off pick-a-back by Self

(That mis-shaped minor devil in the play
With strong, foul stink and flaysome grin

Who leaps on stage to grab his own
In smoke and thunder of the final act)

And dumped then in the midst of desolation,
Utterly alone, where there is neither beast

Nor birdsong, no leaf, no shade, no water,
And no redemption save

Through the miraculous daring
(Is it only a mirage,

The flickering horizon?)
Of the frail, unbidden dove.

SILENCE

We have quarrelled before, and parted. But
Even as she flounced out, slamming the door,
I knew I should come home some day to find
Her repossessing her abode, the rooms
Filled suddenly with light again and laughter.

Not this time, though. This time
There were no high words, only the scowl
And scorn of her averted face. Stale smoke,
Slopped tea, an unmade bed: I frowst here
In the gloom, half-hoping still the phone might ring.

LIMBO
(1991)

Always you must have Ithaca in mind.
Arrival there is your predestined end.
—C.P. Cavafy, 'Ithaca'

SHROUDED COAST

Fend off those shades. They throng my dreams
With their high incessant chatter
Crowding round the trench or crouch like dogs
On all fours lapping up the blood.

It is not these that I would parley with,
But lost companions whose luck ran out:
Who even in the ribald fellowship
Of youth suddenly fell silent

Or vanished overboard without a cry
At midnight in mid-sea—pioneers
So far ahead I cannot read
Their signals now, much less interrogate

Them on this leafless, fog-bound shore.

DONEGAL

Look, this land, mist-shawled
Mostly, earth and sea and sky
A monochrome grey wash,
Is Midas-touched by spring,
Its ragged banks and boreens
Burgeoning gold: how soon spent
In wild profligacy of wind and rain.

ELDER STATESMAN

He was shopping, he said, leaning on his stick,
For his wife, who seldom ventured out these days.
I too had my instructions and a list
Of small necessities. We stood on the corner
While others—women mostly—hurried past,
Heads down, ignoring him, and talked of times gone by

And the evils fallen since upon the city:
Ancient codgers on the walls of Troy
Peering into the dusk and smoke and din,
The confused carnage on the plain below.

ROBIN AMONG SUMMER VISITORS

Connoisseur of bread crumbs and grilled bacon rind,
He would materialise through fog and frost,
Wolf-light of the slinking dawn, with a sudden
Blink of wings outside the kitchen window,
Red kerchief slashed, pirate-fashion, round his neck.
A swivel of head and eye, a few brisk bobs,
And he was gone, to gorge or shelter God knows where.

Occasional accomplices apart—deft
Milk-bottle-raiding blue tits, the whole gang
Hooked on cream—he had the place all winter through
Almost to himself. Yet, so deafening the din
The squatters make these mornings crowded here
Within his tenement, he can't be seen
Or heard. Globetrotters, they will migrate with the sun

Soon enough. But will he swagger back then, buccaneer,
Chest puffed out, ready to defy the dark again?

NEW MANAGEMENT

The rooms were empty but the lights still on.
They had retouched the ceilings, moved the portraits round,
I noticed; but the tables, books, the leather chairs
And velvet draperies were much as I had found

Them years before—that slightly faded opulence,
The silence tingling with expectancy.
A woman entered whom I didn't know,
Sat behind the desk, and startled to see me,

'Yes?' she said. 'Can I help you?' 'Thank you,' I replied,
'I'm waiting for your colleague to appear,'
And mentioned the name. 'There must be some mistake,'
She said. 'There's nobody of that name here.'

'Nobody of that name here? Oh, come,' I said.
She bristled. 'Either you have picked the wrong address,
Or else this ... this person that you speak of left
A long time since—under the old regime, I'd guess.'

'Old regime? What do you mean, the old regime?
And who are you?' I asked. 'Look. You'd better go,'
She said, and rang a bell. 'You weren't invited
And clearly you've no business here. This man will show—'

I'd turned already, blundering through the marble hall
And out. I had found the place again, no question,
Whatever that strange woman may have said:
But far too late—usurpers in possession,

The godhead overthrown, the sibyl fled.

SCHOOL PHOTOGRAPH

Head prefect, captain of the First XI,
He lounges there, athlete, aesthete, all the rage
In Wilde as wit, or Shakespeare as tragedian,
Presaging triumph on the West End stage,
And smiles into the future. Nathaniel
To his Berowne, gawky, shy,
Too easily put down, I recollect
Chiefly now his arrogance and vanity—
And seeing him later once on television
In a minor role, by younger men outshone.
He must be somewhere still, still craving stardom's call.

TRYST

Wind frets the low peninsula,
Scuffs pools, rubs cheekbones raw. Gulls screech,
Red-eyed, and squabble over small
Pickings on a bladderwrack-strewn shore

That shelves to mud. I crunch dry sticks
Along the strand, waiting for the faint
Susurrus in the distance, glint
And ripple of the tide that lifts

Stranded boats off their beam-ends,
Encircles islands, fills the creeks.
When will it fetch you shimmering in
To repossess your precincts,

Bring the bee-delighting scents
And stir of summer once again?

TYNAN

However slow its onset, catastrophe
Is always swift and ruthless at the last.
Night still, no stars; a sudden frenzied din,
Shrieking, sobbing, battery, conflagration,
Then silence: Troy, Mycenae, Tiryns dust

And rubble. O yes, it has happened before.
So, its harvest gathered, last thanksgiving said,
Long shadows of a late October sun
Wheeling across its lawns, this great house waited
For its end. Axes hacking down the door

That moonless night, shouts, shots, old man and his son
Dead in their blood, flames roaring through the roof—
All this was nothing new. The distant pyre
Signalled an ancient order's immolation,
The killers cockroaches scurrying from its glare.

LONG-DISTANCE COACH STATION

They fetch us back, familial errands,
Only to find how much we knew has changed.
I remember this soot-stained city, its grime
So deeply ingrained then that wind and rain

Could never scrub its stony visage clean.
Today its rectangles of shining glass and steel
Focus a fierce Italianate sun
Strayed somehow too far north. Passing through,

I pick my way by instinct more than knowledge
Down half-forgotten streets, past bare-legged girls

Cool in cotton, navvies stripped down to the waist,
To reach this stifling rendezvous, where I arrive

With hours to spare, and nothing to read or do
But wait for evening when the traffic melts
Towards the cooling suburbs; and then last coaches come
Swinging in from London, Glasgow, Birmingham

With a blast of diesel fumes, a sudden cough
And spasm of engines spluttering to a stop.
Their passengers descend, are met with smiles,
Hugs, kisses, by mums, dads, husbands, boyfriends, wives,

Excited children; and, baggage seized, are whisked
To waiting cars that speed into the dusk.
I watch them go, who have no part in these
Small celebrations of love and joy

By strangers in a near-strange place. But that such rites
Are ageless is a consolation,
Let chance demit, time topple what it will.
Yes, even if (here's my lift now) those I attend

These days so rarely signify reunion,
So frequently farewell.

IN A LARGE GREEK COLONY: 200 BC
from Cavafy

That things aren't what they should be in the Colony
There remains not the slightest doubt. Possibly—
For all that we edge forward still somehow—
The time has come, as not a few think now,
To bring in a political reformer.

Yes. But the snag, the difficulty
Is that they make such a self-righteous fuss and stir,
These reformers, over every single thing.
(What a relief, what a blessing it would be
If they were never needed.) They pry
Into the smallest detail, prod and poke, essay,
And radical redispositions spring
At once to mind, to be pursued without delay.

Besides, they have a bent for sacrifice.
'Rid yourselves of that particular property.
Your occupation of it's insecure.
(Just such possessions undermine a colony.)
Abdicate your revenues from this
And from that other source. They're both impure.
Yes, and from this third, which follows naturally.
You need them, do you say? Don't be too sure.
They are a noxious responsibility.'

Then, as they prosecute their audit
They find more superfluities to cut—
Things hard for men, however, to forego.

And when, having finished at last, the whole show
Docketed in detail, all pared down to the bone,
They depart, taking the rewards that are their due,
We'll see what little's left, how small the residue
After such heroic surgery.

                    Well,
Perhaps the time hasn't yet quite come,
We mustn't panic. It is dangerous to rush.
Premature measures soon invite repentance. Sadly,
And certainly, much is wrong in the Colony.
But is there anything human free from blemish?
And after all, we do inch forward (don't we?) still.

INNER CITY

How it blows, skimming salt-marsh, slobland,
Green-ribbed rock, this bleak wind off the sea,
That rifles wharf and warehouse, splatters spray
On silent quays, rattles windows, smashes slates,
Rolls dustbins round back yards, lifts curtains, slams
Doors shut: blusters, sobs, blowing through small

Moon-blanched hours like desolation
Through the derelict, depopulated
Wastes within where once were cafés, shops,
Couples sauntering beneath the lights
Of tree-lined avenues at dusk;
And in the suburbs only yesterday
New blossom, songburst, riot of spring.

FINAL ACT

The game is up, the handcuffs on, stalls and pit
Await the curtain. What can he do but go
Quietly, this wild-eyed creature cornered so
Among his crimes? ('Come along, sir, now. We don't
Want to disturb the neighbours, do we, or
Frighten the kiddies at this hour of night?
Of course not, sir.') Yes, he's got his man, this gaunt
Black-booted emissary of the Law
Whose deadpan entrance always stops the show.

HALLOWE'EN

Beautiful pale girls whose copper hair
Cascades round their shoulders, trees in the park
Stand motionless at dusk. Far south-west the sun
Founders in a burst of sudden fire

That burnishes the city, then smoulders out.
In shops and offices the lights flick on
To ward off ghosts this night the earth exhales
Its dead, and spirits wander. I walk

Past disused bandstand, stripped flowerbed
In mist and silence here towards the gate
Where traffic churns, millracing through the falls
Beyond, and booming in the distance.

What if I should meet you even yet,
Walking towards me, smiling, summers since?

LOVERS

Deciphering the manuscripts exhumed
From centuries of dust and silence, scholars
Noted that her name, so vividly invoked
In the beginning, faded and then vanished
From later scrolls. Cooling passions, some estrangement,
A final rift that parted them for good?
So most commentators plausibly conjecture.
And yet it's possible, just possible

(Even against the odds such things can happen)
That they might have settled, the two of them,
For Roman domesticity: plump matron now
In middle age, paterfamilias weighed down
By paunch and jowl and gravitas. But then
One poem predicates she died still young and rose
From her ashes to taunt and haunt him. Well,
Who knows? Theses will be written yet,
Don will dispute with don. Early or late,
Together or alone, they ended, doubtless
In a mess, shipwrecked like the rest of us.

HOMAGE TO THE BARD

Whose poems run straight
and thin as drainpipes
down the page, flushing
memories of the da,
dead in exile, and
the fiddle-playing uncle
who stored pikes in the thatch
at home, and helped the lads
send old Sir John's place up
one night in flames—only
nobody let on
then, you see, for fear
the peelers in
big shiny boots
would come and get them.
And it all slurps down, seeping
into the Great Bog
where the consciousness
of the race lies hidden
which the bovine Brits
and Prods, who don't belong,
can't find or fathom
ever, no matter how
they rampage round
and wreck the place. And Christ,
it's gloomy there
and rough as hell up here:
though sometimes
there's that girl again

with the wild dark eyes,
the lustrous hair
and delectable breasts
to take his mind off things.

CRETAN MANTINADA

Rank, riches, fame I never envied—
Only a limber frame, a cool, clear head.

AGE

Is crossing the Mall or Aldersgate
Before a wild stampede of traffic, mind
Signalling 'Move': only to find
You don't in fact accelerate.

PROGENY

His dreaming head, beached high and dry at dawn
Among the salt-bleached spars and bladderwrack,
Lifts, squinting at the whale-backed monsters torn
Through gates of ivory—or gates of horn.

TALKING HEAD

It isn't just what fills the frame or box—
The smile, the hairdo—that you ought to watch,
But the mirthless eyes that give away the show,
The flick knife glinting in the fist below.

LEADER OF MEN

Strange how they foundered under him, each ship
In turn, all hands lost save one. As they sank
He bobbed up like a cork among the wreckage,
Gathering glory, medal ribbons, rank;
While in green darkness down below, his crews,
Open-mouthed but mute, rolled helpless at the news.

OLD MAN SITTING IN THE PARK

To renounce the world is one thing:
To be abandoned by it quite another.

NATURAL HISTORY

'The spiders hidden in high places here
Are weaving treason. We're flies caught in their trap,'
You cry. But then, they'd never cock things up
Like this, those subtle spinners you so fear.
No. When ignorance and folly squat
Like toads on top, arachnids scuttle clear.

TRADING STATION

Blown off course, storm-battered and leak-sprung,
He limped ashore in this Phoenician town
Whose quays and alleys teeming morning fills
With street cries, cart, swart foreign seamen jabbering
Among the bales and cordage: where heat bangs down
Like a dustbin lid at noon, clamping the din,
The sizzling flies, fish heads, straw, and smells
Of rotting fruit and garbage tight within.

Through the silence then of shuttered afternoon
Gold light filters onto golden skin
And shadowed eyes. He spends his manhood here
Whose business lies in distant waters, beached
In this creek of time, her salted mouth,
The scented whorls and sea-lift of her hair.

WHAT'S WRONG WITH ABERYSTWYTH?
*'His first lectureship at Aberystwyth (about as inappropriate
a place as possible) was followed ... by a fellowship at Balliol.'*
—Book review in *The Spectator*

When she was twenty-one, Aunt Bertha—
Long before you were born, she used to say,
Spreading the tablecloth, her dimpled face
Beaming at her brother's three small children

(She would have given us anything
If ever she'd had anything to give
But hugs and smiles and home-made cake and jam)—
Went to Aberstwyth for a holiday.
She stayed there for a week in a boarding house
Just behind the seafront, the only time
She ever left home or was waited on.
And coming from the mills, the slag heaps, moors,
The cobbled streets and smoke-grained terraces
Of Lancashire, she thought the place was paradise.

PRE-RETIREMENT COURSE

Solon, the Athenian,
Gave himself, his life's work done,
To pleasure the prerogative
Of youth—wine, music, love;
And yet another handsome boy
Was Pindar's geriatric joy.

Pray, gentlemen, don't emulate
These carnal follies of the great
And good. They'd never do, such goings-on,
In Bath or Budleigh Salterton;
And think of the wagging hats, the shame
And outrage over tea in Cheltenham.

There's worse to come. You still can't live
Life backwards crowned with vine or olive—
No, not even in the bright Aegean.

THE COMMISSARS CONFIRM THEIR SHORT LIST

Yes, these are the big names. In their cots
They strangled snakes. Childhood and youth
Were full of portents; they came down
With Firsts in almost everything,
Famous already, then took the town
By storm. Yes, these are the big shots
Everybody's heard of. They will run—
Always to tumultuous applause—
A lyric sprint or prose-packed marathon

At the drop of a chequebook any day
In record time to grab the prize.
They're also good at gouging eyes
And kicking shins. (Why not, when they
Pick the ref and mostly write the laws?)

The rest are nameless, undefined
Except by what they're not: unplaced
Among the halt, the lame, the blind.
They'll never make the grand tour east
Of the Graeco-Roman cities, pack
The amphitheatre in Antioch
Or Ephesus. True, some might be sent
Where no one else will go—to Pontus,
Say, or Bactria maybe, where
They're glad of anybody, too uncouth
To notice lapses of deportment,
Unmodish manners, rustic training.
What might pass there would never do
For cultivated taste, or qualify
For Panhellenic sponsorship
Anywhere that matters ...

Posterity?
Sod posterity. We shan't be here
When out of this whole rabblement
It disinters the real right thing.

AGE OF HEROES

O the afternoons of those wet Saturdays
In winter when we scuffled in the queue,
Then, slapping tuppence down, pushed and squeezed into
The tight-packed dark, ducking the missiles hurled
By rough boys at the back with gobstoppers
And bottles of exploding pop. How we'd cheer
And stamp when faithful Rin Tin Tin escaped at last
To warn his master, who, gun belt buckled on,
The deputy's tin star pinned on his chest,
Strode into the town's main street (suddenly
Unpeopled now) where bad men always bit the dust.

Childish, yes. But how many times since then
Have we stepped forth to knock some villain flat

In fantasy, with one contemptuous blow
Avenging private snub or public wrong—
The crowd acclaiming us, the hitherto
Far princess of our most lascivious dreams
Gasping her gratitude and admiration?
A pity life so rarely matches art:
That great Achilles broods still in his tent
Unrecognised, while boors and braggarts grab the spoils
Of Troy, the gorgeous diadems, the scented girls.

RIBBLESDALE

Like the flash of a kingfisher's wing
Skimming down some deep-shadowed stream
You dart into my memory, deft
And witty and delightful, a quick
Bright presence glimpsed again then gone.
No, not gone. Vivid, distant as a dream
The pebbled rivers, woods, the golden haze
Enfolding us that summer afternoon
We walked by Dinckley to Hurst Green.

ST. JAMES'S, PICCADILLY

I

Wealth and fashion once adorned this church
For matings mostly, yes, but matins too,
Behind gloved hand or silken cuff and lace
Discreetly yawning through a Sunday sermon.

From elegant town house, from noble square,
Sinners of this parish everyone,
Or masters of many acres in the shires
And mistresses of country mansions come

With lady's maids and footmen, children, coachmen,
Cooks, to London for the season,
They entered here a rational universe
Of order, harmony, proportion

Grander by far than anything they knew
Yet still familiar: its lucid mystery

Prefigured in resplendent light,
Common day a sudden glory, golden, white.

II

Migrants seeking refuge from the roar
And gabble of a gross cosmopolis,
We flop down each in turn, two or three
Gathered together here in no one's name,

One resting old bones at the back, one
In seeming contemplation, a third in shorts
And open shirt, guidebook in hand, staring
At this late Carolingian masterpiece

Encased in sooty brick. Where have you absconded,
God? To what black hole beyond the galaxies,
What dim, deserted shrine where goat tracks cross
The mountain path, and snuffed cold candles splay,

And faded saints look down from flaking walls?
You give no sign. Incongruously lest
My steps disturb your silence, I tiptoe out,
One of the not-quite-unbelievers who

Drop small coins in the box beside the door
With the hollow clunk of metal upon wood
To ward off evil, assuage guilt; and so retreat
To the apophatic theology of the street.

MR. CAVAFY'S BYZANTINE ARCHON VERSIFYING IN HIS EXILE

'Conventional stuff,' you say,
'Boring too—strict metre, rigid form,
Pompous, frigid as the man himself.'
Well, perhaps it kept the slinking wolf
That preyed on his small hours at bay,
This candle guttering through night and storm.

LAST NIGHT

Last night I saw you in my dreams again.
People were gathering, strangers mostly,
In some grand hall for cocktails before dinner,
Bejewelled, decorated, all in evening dress—
I among them, glass in hand, nodding, smiling,
Eyes ransacking the room for you in vain.

At table, then, one chair stood empty. At last
You came, charming the host with your apology
As you passed towards your place, your words
In that musical low voice I knew so well
Exciting laughter and applause. Avidly
I searched your face. You were hardly changed: no older
Certainly, more beautiful than ever,
Absorbed, it seemed, in conversation
With your attentive neighbours on each side.
Not knowing how to meet your gaze, I was afraid
That soon your glance might fall on me. But no.
You neither looked nor offered any sign
Of recognition, removed into a world
Not mine. I sat there, lips, mouth, dry, exalted
As always in your presence yet dismayed ...

Then woke, shuffled round the bed, drew the curtains
Back. It was four o'clock: a long while before dawn.

MEDIZERS

They were rational men, the Medizers,
Not xenophobic or hysterical,
Their policy grounded firmly in self-interest—
To keep clear of a war they couldn't win
Against the Great King's overwhelming might
On land and sea. How could the Spartans, stubborn,
Arrogant as ever, hold Thermopylae
With a mere three hundred men and a rabble
Of helots and some half-trained hangers-on?
Athens too, all big talk since Marathon
And empty gestures—you'd see how soon her ships
Would cut and run for home when things got rough,
As they surely would, of Artemision.

There was no salvation from such quarters. No.
The one way of averting futile slaughter
Was to offer earth and water to the Mede
In token of submission, make a show
Of welcome, and save whatever could be saved
By bribery and diplomatic skill.

                              Thus
The Medizers, whom history consigned,
Knowing which side won, to obloquy.
They are still around today, realists
Counselling compromise and caution,
Men comfortably off with much to lose
Like their predecessors in that hot, dry spring.
Now, informed observers everywhere commend
Their moderation and good sense: not so
The creatures trapped here in the labyrinth,
Enemy or friend, who stumble through the common dark
Towards what glint of light, what sudden, squalid end?

CROSSINGS

It always started after dark, that journey,
Mostly in the dead of winter when
The boat train pulled out on its long haul north:
Slowed at last, jolting through junctions, clanked
And squealed then to a halt beside the quay
Past midnight, a keen wind whisking clouts of steam
Up beyond the lamplight. Stubbing cigarettes
Or yawning in the fug, the passengers
Struggled into coats, stuffed magazines away,
Reached luggage down, and stumbled out, straggling
Through muddy sheds towards the ship's black bulk
Bunched high above her moorings, the oily glint
Of sluggish water heaving in the dock.

        The harbour lights recede, the last
        Cold whimpers of a dying gale
        Fret in the rigging. Against
        Our rusty sides the flick and flash
        Of a lighthouse beam through darkness
        Swinging from unseen cliffs, the lift
        And slap, hiss and slobber
        Of the dream-tossed, paroxysmal sea,

The vessel booming, lurching through the night
Towards what landfall in the leaden murk
Of dawn, what gull-screams out of desolation?

Fitful sleep of slamming doors, sliding crates,
A drumming deck, woke to a horizon
Bleak enough: a long dark coast
Opening in the half-light massive jaws
Of black-fanged rock; then smudge of grey on either bow
Converging into mud banks, gantries, wharfs;
And cloaked in cloud, a raw and windy city
Raising blinds on puddled streets, another day.

This, then, is how it was, or seemed to be.
What rites of passage had we undergone?
What judgment, death, what strange rebirth?
How much was real, how much hallucination,
Or some kind of foreknowledge? We stepped ashore,
Each to his appointed end, head down,
Coat collar turned in the quotidian rain.

POLONIUS COMPLAINS
'he's for a jig or a tale of bawdry, or he sleeps'

It's not the spells of dullness or mere vacancy
That fret me most, dimmed sight, decay of powers.
At my age, one nods off all too easily.
No. It's the gabble of night voices in my head
Crackling through static: some mad insomniac
Who squats there in the dark, hours upon hours
Twiddling the wavebands of the set beside my bed.

SATAN'S ADVICE

Let it cohabit, this animal,
Together with the female of its kind
For weeks or months within a space confined
To them alone, called Paradise. They'll soon lust
For something new, surrounded by the dull
Scratched shards of boredom, bickering, disgust.

STAFF PARTY

She looked experienced as well as pretty.
I clowned a while and told my favourite jokes.
(One thing I said I really thought quite witty.)
She smiled, it's true, but didn't seem impressed
Till somebody mentioned Smyth. I pictured Smyth—
We all knew Smyth—him of the wheezy chest,
The woollen cardigan and grizzled head,
Old Granny Smyth, who never would
Be manager of this or any store.
'Oh, but I think he's wonderful,' she said,
Cheeks aglow, eyes shining. 'Tell me more.'

OLYMPIC GAMES

Afterwards, did he boast, say he was sorry
Like some, or simply withdraw without a word,
Leaving the girl to make up her own story
For scandalised ears, while back at home, bored
With the wife, he pictured how he would discharge
Himself on the next innocent at large?

APPARITION

'Fuckin' foreigner,' he said, his pale, mad face
Thrust into mine. 'Get to fuck out of Ulster.'
He had heard me exchange greetings—nothing more—
With an acquaintance passing in the street
Thronged with traffic: leapt forward and was gone,
Loping towards the Markets or Short Strand,
Before I could begin to gather myself.
Well over twice his age, I had lived here,
Worked here, longer by far than my assailant.
This was home ...

                    And yet it was the sting
Of truth within his venom stopped me short.
For him and his kind I am the enemy
To be driven out, the scapegoat for all sins
Whose going will bring peace and brotherhood
Throughout the land. So they say, killing the while

Those they call their countrymen who happen still
To disagree.

                    What kinship can I claim
With the dissenters then? Another landscape,
Other weathers—mist and lough and mountain,
Drumlin, rock, the soughing rain—bent, moulded them
To psalm and Sabbath, field and byre and farmstead,
Clipped of speech, in a land of talkers taciturn
Keepers of counsel, cleaving to their gods.
A stubborn race, their virtues out of fashion,
Who will memorialise them now
That Hewitt's dead, and I a metic in their midst?

INSOMNIA

Last night I laid an ambush
To check your lodgement in my heart
And drive you from my head.
The poor ruse failed. Instead
You wound more deeply in my brain
And took possession of my heart
By right of conquest once again.
My love, why do you always thus
Invade each night my drunken heart
Yet still abjure my bed?

METAMORPHOSIS
vera incessu patuit dea

Tall, grey-eyed, she moved through summer with the lithe
Grace of an Athena in her elegant
Simplicity of sandalled foot and dress:
Then vanished, a remembered vision,

Only to reappear beneath the lamps
Of autumn, now with lipsticked mouth,
Blue-shadowed eyelids, hobble skirt and high
Black heels, her bangles, beads and earrings
Jingling like some tart's on a street corner
As she stepped out of the shadows, Aphrodite
Confronting my astounded gaze.

CELTIC BARD, BURGHER'S WIFE

Grizzled, broke, with a small child's grasping hands
And greedy mouth, he rolled his beer-blown gut
From pub to pub round Soho, from pub to party
At one of which they met. A plain Dutch mare
Turned skittish, she jumped her fences, fled the Netherlands
To join him for a passionate affair
In distant Ireland. But then unending rain,
Stale smells of cabbage lingering on stair
And corridor, a loudly creaking bed,
The landlady's cold sniff and shake of head
Fetched her in a few weeks home again
To level ways, those sober rich interiors
The Flemish master knew. What next? That bird, maybe,
Above? The one in Barons Court? He's free
To prey once more for bed, booze, board: or worse,
He'll fornicate and multiply in verse.

REMORSE

Oh no: that it should come to this,
Such ruin, wrack, and bitterness
Between us two, all noxious, overgrown.
What serpent slid into our garden
With his false heart and subtle tongue
And curled about you with a hiss
And smile? So guileless they seemed then,
That smile, that kiss, how could you have known
They hid my crooked heart, my flickering tongue.

GEROUSIA

The first bright day of spring draws them out again,
Hobbling on their sticks into the park
To warm old bones, and watch excited dogs
And children chase each other across lawns.
It is colder than they think. The daffodils
Have not yet lifted, some of them, their heads
Even in this sun, but shiver in the wind
As these upon their benches now, huddled here
In coats and caps and scarves. 'Bit chilly still,'

I say, nodding as I pass. They grunt or nod
In turn, sparing speech. A year or two and I
Shall take my seat in their laconic council.

DOMESTIC INTERIOR

Winter kills them off, old dog, old people,
Who once rebuffed its random malice
But have no stomach left now for a fight.
I wake, counting the chimes of a church steeple,
As usual at four, and blink to find
The room blanched with reflected light
Of newly fallen snow. A rising wind
Riffles through hedges as a conjurer
Riffles cards. Small creatures, birds and mice,
Snuggle against the cold as best they can.
Below, dog sprawled before a long-dead fire
Mumbles, stirs, slumps stiffly in his basket.
I pulled the bedclothes round my neck. In heat
Of blood, shudder of tumescence, we began.

OVERTURE AND BEGINNERS

Beware the curse of general praise
That flatters, soon grows sated, then betrays
To contumely. Better by far endure
Neglect, whose stony places sometimes flower.

THE OTHER KINGDOM

Winter would be worst, I thought, its wild storms
Lashing your grave and beating down your flowers,
The byways blocked by snow, ice crusting ruts and mire,
Even your name, all that's still left of yours.
But I'd not bargained for your loveliness
In spring: primrose, daffodil and whin
A glory of sudden gold and green
In hedge, in hollow. To see you everywhere
Yet never to find you, this
Stabs the heart, is sharpest anguish.

ZOO

They screech and gibber, scutter, scratch and stink,
Kick, bite, claw for place and precedence
In snatching food or females; are groomed for fleas,
Assert their primacy with screams of rage.

It isn't mere hallucination
By hypoglycaemia induced or drink,
Nor yet the mordancy of shipwrecked age
That peoples streets with apes, baboons and monkeys

While gentle creatures languish in the cage.

WHITE CHURCH AT BALLINTOY
haec porta domini; justi intrabunt in eam

The village lines the coastal road, a thin
Straggle, Irish fashion, of houses, pubs,
Small shops, cottages: yet tidy, touched no doubt
By the Scottish passion for cleanliness
And order. A mile beyond, across broad fields
That slope towards the sea, the church stands on the edge
Of the escarpment, a solitary keep
In this treeless landscape tall, commanding
In the distance. But then, close by
It dwindles to squat tower, blunt nave,
Its whitewash flaked blue-grey, a low stone wall
Crooked around its dead, in hummocked earth
Patiently awaiting resurrection.

I try the door, which yields, and entering find
All seemly, plain within, quite unmistakeably
Anglican in the Hibernian mode
Outcropped here among the deep
Striated seams that riddle this rock-bound coast,
The world's end once, whose massive boreal headlands
Rebuff the North Atlantic's fling and fury.
But not today. Today a slumbering sea
Nuzzles the tiny harbour down below.
Due north, Islay and the Paps of Jura
Smudge the far horizon, which kindles briefly now
Far in the west, then smoulders like snuffed wick. Fleeting

As a gull's faint cry that fades into the dusk
Across these great grey waters, the hungers
Here of flesh, blood's fever, heart's delirium
Are gathered into solitude and silence
With all the generations gone before.

In the decaying light of late November
I have come here craving commerce with the dead.
Along the empty pews my footsteps echo
Hollowly on wood. Not meaning to, I sink
On stiff and unaccustomed knees, old man,
Who finds no words that can articulate,
Or prayer appease, the dog's howl of his grief.

LIMBO

The track ends here in reeds, and fog
And silence. Nothing stirs.
There is no way forward, no way back:
Nothing to do but wait, to listen

For muffled voices, the creak
And splash of oars, a keel
Grating on shingle. Or possibly
Tomorrow or the next day, or the next

Again, the wind may rise, cleansing
Vision for a moment to reveal
A foundered sun, gouting smoke and fire
Beyond the desolate horizon

And on the far shore mud banks, marshland, dull
Miasma of corruption and despair.

NEW & UNPUBLISHED POEMS
(1991-1995)

HALF-REMEMBERED THINGS

My brother dead, they hold no interest now,
These half-remembered things, for anyone but me.
I rummage through the boxes where he kept them,
Custodian of the family's few records
Deposited at random, relegated now
To disused attics—old photographs in sepia,
Letters in faded ink, cuttings curled like leaves
Yellowing in autumn from journals long defunct.

So, here's my mother in a long silk gown,
Tall, dark-haired and slim, holding my brother
As a baby in her arms, the first-born son
Who brought such wonder and fulfilment; my sister
With a ribbon in her hair, tied in a large bow;
My school report in the scholarship class, aged 10,
Endorsed by my father in his firm, clear hand;
All five of us, a formal family group.

I gather them together once again,
The shadows and the words on crinkled paper
Sorted into bundles. The household gods
Are homeless now, their dwelling up for sale.
They will all go with me then, last of the line,
To Ireland briefly among strangers there.
And when I die, they will go with me too
Into oblivion, that silence where

All will be at last, at last at home.

YOUNG MAN AND OLD

Don't grind your teeth, cantankerous old fool.
Think of something pleasant you might say
For once, some quip, some tale to cheer us up.

I'm not yet so senile that I drool
And grin through every dreary, witless day,
Or cackle as I lift the poisoned cup.

Count your small blessings, lad. Who else would rage
That you, not I, must suffer this filthy age?

A TOAST
to Mr. George Morrow on his birthday

Here's to George, who as a lad
Stumped the country with his dad
And wicked uncles; set the stage
For their performance, all the rage,
Of plays like *Thompson in Tir-na-nog*,
Whose fame leapt mountain, stream and bog
To please both Orange and Free Stater,
The Ulster Lit'rary Theatre.

Then, almost fifty years ago
George co-inspired another show
Called the Masquers, whose repertory
Stretched from Mizen Head to Tory.
Comedy, tragedy, or farce,
Demotic prose or high-flown verse,
Home or away, whatever the plot
Twenty years on they'd read the lot,
Drama then gave place to art, new ways
Of staging exhibitions, not plays.
Next they took to dining-out and chat,
Things even they admit they're good at;
And if perhaps a little deaf,
And by the sere and yellow leaf
Tinged these days, they're going strong
Still the fallen world among.

So here's to George, the master craftsman,
Sculptor, stage-designer, draughtsman,
Raconteur, and inspiration
As domine for half the nation,
Co-founder of Tomorrow's Press
With Faye as his amanuensis—
Of New Year, 1995
Many Happy Returns, George. May you thrive.

A MEMORIAL FOR MY SISTER

I was the best toy my sister ever had,
Better even than her favourite dolly.
Whatever she told me to do, I'd do
(Though very timid) without hesitation

And in perfect health. All the games we played
She invented. On solemn Sunday afternoons
Confined in winter to the house, she'd find some way
To break the boredom, if only by teasing me

With stratagems I never saw through—that song
About a robin redbreast in the snow
Which always made me blubber; plucked tomato top
Dropped on my plate with cries of 'Spider, spider'

To startle me at table; open umbrella
Twirled like a giant mushroom in my face
Which had me howling. Yet if I lost a fight
When rough lads swarmed in clogs across the tip

Flinging stones and hunting for a victim
Among the cissies of our genteel neighbourhood,
It was she who rescued me and then pretended
I had won. If I wouldn't go to bed,

Frightened of the dark, she'd go with me and we'd talk
Through the open doors of our adjoining rooms,
Snug and secure, till slumber overcame us.
Chock-full in childhood of vitality

And mischief, disruptor of domestic peace,
She grew in gentleness and love, cherishing
My mother to the end; then struggled for years, slumped
Dead in her pew one night in church. Spoilt kid brother

Who took far more than he gave, old man now I set
These things down while there's still time, redeeming time
As best I can: a few bedraggled flowers
For a distant, unregarded grave.

CLOSED SHOP

Senior retired civil servants
Collect directorships today
And write their memoirs—extended pre-
Obituary notices
Concocted by the corpse-to-be
Alas, it never came my way
Boardroom bliss, the perks, the pay,
But memoirs ... ? They're another game
Entirely I could play,
Fudging guilt, shifting the blame
For what went wrong, where and when,
And cultivating the pure flame
Of spotless reputation. Then
Think of the famous men I knew
Whose names I could discreetly drop,
A salty anecdote or two
To raise a smile or lift the veil
On folly ... Yes, it might just do
Somewhere else. Not here. Who here could gloss
The deadly tedium of our deadly tale?

A WOMAN OF NAZARETH

'Is not this the carpenter, the son of Mary?'

O yes, we sniggered at her pregnancy,
Neighbours and noseyparkers, all agog
At her girth. 'So, there's life in the old man yet,'
We said, 'or else some tinker on his rounds last spring
Gave her what she fancied in the fields
Beyond the town.' 'Or maybe one of us obliged,'
Young louts guffawed, nudging each other, winking.
'Anyway, who does she think she is, Mistress High
And Mighty,' the women said, 'keeping herself
To herself, with never a word or smile
For anyone—the Queen of Sheba?'

Then rumours filtered down from Bethlehem
Of strange events the night that she gave birth
In (what a comedown for her) a stable
Behind some rowdy pub among beasts stinking

In their stalls and drunkards stumbling through the yard
To urinate, cursing as they fell. Later—
And I can only tell you what I have seen
Or heard for myself, a respectable woman
Getting on in years—later there was talk
Of three mysterious foreigners—kings.
Some said—who came out of the east with costly gifts
And knelt before the child, still then in this manger.

Yet, when at last they brought the baby home.
She and her husband, she seemed much more at ease,
So taken with her child, showing him off, gossiping
With other women, exchanging recipes
And simple remedies for small upsets
And cuts and bruises, contentedly
Absorbed in household cares and duties. As for him,
He was what he always had been: a quiet,
Hard-working man who gave offence to none.

As the boy grew, though, some things about him
Troubled his parents: powers of mind,
Leaps of thought beyond their comprehension
Or his years: sometimes a sudden glance
That went straight through them, leaving nothing hid;
Long silences, as if he were listening
To a far voice no-one else could hear. They knew then
His father's trade would never hold him, or any trade
Found in these dusty streets and alleyways
Where we too played as children and shuffle through now
In age. He will move on, no question—to what
Exalted place among his people, what bad end?

CAMOUFLAGE

Most strip down well in youth,
Gymnasts, say,
With rippling muscles
Delighting in their self-display.

For the old and gnarled and bent
Or gross and squat
Undressing is humiliation
Even in private.

From their own and the world's eye
Some have Savile Row, some M&S,
Some mink, some marquessates, some
Rags to hide their nakedness.

It makes no odds. They all
Like beaten dogs limp trembling home.

BALLYMACARRETT BLUES: SUMMER 1994

'They'll soon be dancing on our graves you'll see.'
'Yes, and raping our women. A rampant cock
Is always the victor's prize, while the vanquished
Droop in anguished impotence.'
'Hold on, hold on. This makes no sense.
Their war's not nearly won.' 'Not yet, maybe.
But failing all else, they'll shag their way
Through their own kind to mastery.'

ANCESTRY

A minor setback here and there, a few
Stinging rebukes from the self-righteous,
He soon recovers confidence, old Adam,
Knowing the world is made of the same stuff
That fashioned him, greedy, lecherous and sly,
Snatcher of advantage, sneerer, fleerer 'Sod you,

Jack', and crower on small dungheaps: whom envy gnaws
Of bigger cocks on mightier middens, those
That pull the choicest birds, nick with beak and claw
The fattest grubs. His genes on Saturdays
Throng draughty terraces among the gridded streets
Of Leeds or Liverpool or Tottenham,

Flat caps, raw faces, fags and boozy breath,
Aggression bawling out of 50,000 throats;
Or they gather in Belgravia to scratch
And cackle at a wedding or a dinner
In morning or in evening dress—one big
Worm-eaten family, now and evermore.

PRELUDE

After night's turbulence a silent dawn.
The swarming city slumbers still
As traffic signals blink on empty streets;
And spangled hedges web the breathing fields.

A white mist gathered on the Lough
Will lift, rolled back by the risen sun,
And all the murmuring miles, the creeks and bays
And streaming glens from here to Donegal

Will open flower-like in the golden warmth
Of summer at flood-tide. In truth
It is humanity pollutes this land.
Fox and crow, stoat and cormorant—all these

Are innocent. It is the human heart
That nurtures hate and lusts to main and murder;
The human eye that stalks its victim day
By covert day, patiently to calculate

The perfect place to slaughter. Somewhere today
A drifting cloud of acrid dust
Will settle slowly on disfigured flesh,
The gaping intestinal wounds that spill

Blood and viscera and broken glass
And rubble over road or walk-way. Someone,
Somewhere, observing his handiwork
On TV screen or front-page photograph

Will smirk with satisfaction.

SCRAPHEAP

Never start something that you cannot finish,
My mentors said when I was young. How wise,
I murmured, paying not the slightest heed.
Now, my world is full of uncompleted business,
Abandoned causes, bankrupt companies,
Fragments of poems, plays, failed love-affairs,
Sentences unsaid. Some I launched, it's true,
Soon lost at sea. But almost all were started
By men who never doubted what to do.

SHOREDITCH

Fat she may be and old and gray, no longer a pretty sight.
But lit, she still goes off like a firecracker on Guy Fawkes' night.

MEDICAL WARD

You lie down here with strangers likewise
Stethoscoped, palpated, diagnosed and docketed

Among them late at night the moribund
Whom you know by the commotion round their beds,
The curtains drawn, lights on, whisperings, doctors
And nurses coming and going, relatives
Crumpled on benches in the corridor outside.

Morning brings the convalescents, ward-wise now
Who ride the day's routine with practised ease
And stroll about in dressing-gowns, watch sport
On TV, chaff the nurses, reminisce
Enjoying their short lease of idleness.

The rest of us lie supine, bedfast still,
Shrivelled and inert, and wondering which way
And when we might depart this place—whether
To the roaring city's smoke again and squalor
Or, after slump and rattle, silence of the Styx.

SUNDAY SERVICE

Through the midlands now on a warm summer's evening
My train clanks and winds, sniffing its cautious way
Across no-man's land pock-marked by foundries, scarred
By scrapyards, where crumbling salients of blackened brick
Drive deep into a stricken countryside.
And jolting through junctions, over arches,
Embankments, I stare a moment into the lives
Of people I shall never meet: a baby
In its father's arms, waving to the train,
Shirt-sleeved men, smoking in their allotments,
Young lovers hand in hand on a green lane.

We gather speed past bowling greens and gardens,
A roadhouse neon-lighted in the dusk,
To plunge into another landscape
Of weathered stone and square clock-towers and steeples
And elm and oak and hedges white with may.
Rattling along in a new-lit box, I watch
What once was England like a stage-set whirled away
As darkness falls, the proscenium a void
Filled only by reflections that sway

And mimic every movement made within. But soon
We slide again past suburbs, sidings, terraces
And squeal then to a halt. A muffled voice
Echoing from the gloomy vault above
Announces our late coming and departure
To the few travellers strewn on platforms there,
Wan faces drained of hope beneath the lamplight.
So, nudging north, we jerk once more towards
A distant terminus. I yawn now, bleary-eyed
Like all the rest, while round us everywhere
From cooling towers and banked-down furnaces
Cities fume in silence for tomorrow,
Incinerating time in their dull glare.

MAKER

They float into the mind
Unbidden, fragments, scraps
Of verse. Where they come from,
What's before or after,
Who can tell? Blind yet, you run
Your hands along the grain,
Testing for direction, feeling
For design, the way
The poem might shape itself.
Now you can do no more
Than ease it into the light
Slowly at first, slowly
Till it suddenly insists
On being born. Praised,
Fussed over, or ignored
There it is, alive
And kicking in the world.

RUE LEPSIUS

'Shall I install electric light,' he said,
'Or shall I move?' He did neither, of course,
Preferring, as always, to savour a choice
Than to act. Besides, the flat had been his home
For many years; and if the street and neighbourhood
Sank ever deeper into squalor, well
'Why should I move when all my needs are met?'
He said—bi-sexual brothel down below,
Orthodox church across the way, a hospital
Of sorts around the corner.

Electric light, then?
Too new still, too brash, too unsparing. Candles
Left pools of darkness which imagination
Could people with events long ago, the shades
Of Myris or of young Caesarion:
Or he himself would sit apart, half-hidden
In the shadow while he scrutinized his guest,
Every line etched by an oil-lamp's glare ...

So,
Noiseless as the Nile, his time slid by. He died
Protesting that the end had come too soon,
Some manuscripts lodged with remaining friends,
Two dozen poems still inside his head.

MAN OF PROPERTY

I had hoped for something more commodious
Than this cramped suburban semi: noble terrace,
Lofty rooms, fine staircases, an ample park
With vistas over wood and stream and hill
Matching the airy elegance within,
The many ingenious lovely things
To captivate the eye and stir the heart.

I chose the site with care. Uncultivated then
It seemed rich, I thought, in promise. But soon
The cash gave out. I put the plans away
And lost them. Then the big boys muscled in,
Developers with diamonds and cigars, who bricked

The whole place over, running up blocks of flats,
Shops, massage-parlours, offices. I could only watch

Squeezed here into my tiny rooms and garden.
To coax a sunless rose, discourage weeds,
Paper over cracks in plaster-work,
Board up broken windows, tidy the shed,
Perhaps, on good days, bed a plant or two,
Is not the life I had envisaged. Still,
It keeps me going, I suppose. And what else could I do?

RECTOR

We sat in the kitchen, four of us,
Drinking wine and eating bread and olives
All strangers to each other save for one
Well-known to the rest, a bulky, genial,
Untidy, white-haired man, prompting great gusts
Of laughter as our animation grew.
'What better way to spend an afternoon,'
He said to our inquiring hostess, briefly
Escaped from other guests about the house,
'Than in good talk, nourished by the only food
Mankind truly needs.'

Yet one passing cloud
Shadowed for a while that sunlit day's
Serenity. 'I am an Irishman,' he said,
'And my father's father and his father too
Were Irishmen, and his again and yet again
For generations more. But down there' (pointing
South) 'they want to be rid of such as me,
The few of us still left—to drive us out
Of our own country. There are more ways, you know,
To kill a cat than by using a shotgun.'

Before the war was out he died, his church
Packed nave and transept for his funeral
By old and young, rich and poor, the halt, lame and blind,
All friends of his. Even the seven deadly sins
That roamed his parish like a rowdy street-gang
Erupting everywhere, fell silent
Out of momentary shame. Earth received him,

But not the place his forbears knew as home
Among the few still left there of his kind.

END OF THE AFFAIR

After much painful cogitation
I have concluded with regret, said he,
That elderly gentlemen should never press
Their still concupiscent attention
On beautiful young women such as you.
I am flattered by your gallantry, said she,
Towards one of riper years. But in the sadness
Of these late summer evenings, let us both eschew
Bare fact, the shock and shame of disillusion.

FIVE CRETAN MANTINADES
and
AN EPIGRAM BY PLATO

They are much alike, Love and Time,
Very much alike these twain.
Both of them pass, and leave behind
Nothing but ruins and pain.

———

How could you have forgotten, cur,
The bitter sweetness, sharp delight
That once we knew, entwined
In one another's arms at night?

———

When I am dead and gone, stay clear of my grave.
Keep off the grass,
Lest I burst into flames again
And scorch you as you pass.

———

Even in the bleakness of despair
Some sprig of hope still clings

As, in a cleft among those barren rocks,
Cyclamen still springs.

———————

As stars begin to tremble when
Dawn's fingers brush the sky,
My heart starts to tremble when,
Fresh as morning, you step by.

———————

You gaze at the stars, my star. Would I were heaven
To gaze at you with a myriad eyes.

LOWER ORDER

I once saw Compton make seventy at Lord's
In less than an hour before lunch. Then
He was bowled. Having compiled three score and ten
By nudges, snicks, singles, never fours
I shall soon depart for the pavilion
To less tumultuous (no doubt) applause.

PLANTER

'O the oak and the ash and the bonny ivy tree
They all flourish at home in my north country'

In a quarter of the garden where other trees
Had failed to take root, my father planted an ash.
It grew tall and slender with a graceful cupola
Each spring and summer of blossom and pale green leaf,
In that high, wild country native and at home.

Years later, visiting my widowed mother—
The ash now spread in full maturity—
I plucked a green shoot springing in its shade
And took the shoot back with me to Ireland
Where I planted it beside my gate. It grew

In another boreal landscape straight
And true, the image of its progenitor,
And stands there still, benign domestic dryad
Protecting the house. It will outlive me
As its forbear has long outlived my father,

Though no doubt a bomb, or a bull-dozer and chain-saw
Would make short work of it. Yet if it dies
In nature, let it not rot within slowly,
Root and branch, but be consumed in a flash,
Thunderbolt-riven still in its late prime.

HARVEST

Age winnows, threshes, blows away the chaff,
The vanities, self-deceptions, lusts, the raw
Cravings of the flesh, the spurious triumphs,
Public honours masking private shame.
What's left then on the marble threshing floor
But a scattering of husks and straw?

EPIPHANY

The first faint stir of life in field and byre
Ruffles the silence of a summer dawn. Soon
The slow drip-drip of traffic in the distance
Will gather to a roar as humankind
Floods back into the city made by man

Creator and destroyer, exalted
And depraved, whose smile conceals the treachery
Of his black heart, whose word deceives, who now,
Secure in its possession, despises
What he once most coveted; twitches

For a while insect-like with lust and then
Is gone. These things are seeded here in time. Yet
For a moment the house breathes peace; and suddenly,
Throats raised as one, all the birds of heaven start to sing.

CHRISTMAS EVE

Glancing up as we climbed into the car,
We saw her hand and arm at the bedroom window
Waving a slow good-bye. Upstairs
We had tried to be bright and talkative.
Did she have many visitors? 'Enough.'
Did she mix much with other residents?
'No. Why should I? They're all derelict like me.
I can put up with myself—I have to
Anyway—but not with them.' Her mordancy
Strangled our banalities at birth
And wrecked—though she meant no harm—a game-plan
Shallow as it was inept. We knew
As we turned to go, presenting a trifling gift
Not to be opened till she woke next day,
And promising to come back very soon,
That we should never see her again—
And so did she, though she left the words unsaid:
Roman matron straight-backed in her chair, her fierce
Dignity of spirit the last redoubt
Of selfhood in this place of desolation.
And then that final gesture from the shades
Under the wheeling, bald, mephitic birds.

ONE OF THE BOYS

I am a freedom-fighter. I kill and maim
To strike power from oppression's palsied hand
And free my country from its foreign yoke.
Tyranny dethroned, the foreigner driven out,
Then (solely to secure the revolution
From the mechanisations of its enemies)
I shall rule, and bend all to my will: for I
Incarnate the people's destiny. Meanwhile
By squeezing the trigger I liberate
You from your errors—you and many more
Who likewise make a feeble, futile stand
Against the flood tide here of history.

LANDSCAPE IN WINTER

How fleeting now, how rare these visitations,
A sudden shaft of sunlight stabbing the dark
Waters of the lough below, then melting,
Vanishing in swirls of mist, the hills
Beyond blacked out by cloud and rain.

THERE ARE MORE THINGS ...

Civilisations have collapsed before
In fire and Blood. What makes you think this one secure?

THE ROUNDABOUT

I have grown more reclusive still with age,
Abandoning the bedlam of the world
For the bedlam in my head—the muttering,
The jeering, fleering, shouting, the cries and sighs,
The trudging through the small hours round my skull,
Lone prisoner in the exercise yard,
Round and round the circuit of despair,
Guilt, grief and rage. To be shadowed everywhere

By half-glimpsed figures lurking in the mind
That sap the will and paralyse decision
Is the curse of my family, inherited
God knows where or when. Death only brings release
For then the blaring roundabout must stop,
The lift and lurch of those grotesque carved creatures cease.

AUNT SISSIE

'They can say what they like about your Sissie,'
My father remarked to my mother in my hearing once
(Aunt Sissie was rather pious, down on drink,
Loose women, all such frailties of the flesh)
'But if ever there's illness in the family
Or any kind of trouble, there she is
With her apron on and her sleeves rolled up,
Ready to help in any way she can.'

Father was right. If one of us went down
With measles, say, or whooping cough, or maybe a real
Child-killer of the age such as diphtheria—
I can still remember how my mother blanched
When she heard that diagnosis—Aunt Sissie
Would materialise next day or the next
Washing, ironing, cooking, scrubbing, polishing.
Keeping the household routines running smoothly
Until the crisis passed, when she would disappear
As quietly as she had come.

Ditched
By her drunken husband years before, Aunt Sissie now
Kept house for her widowed brother, Uncle Jack, M.P.
(No less) for Oldham. We didn't make much,
We kids, of Uncle Jack, whom we seldom saw
Since he spent his time in far off London mostly.
He always spoke with grave deliberation
As if addressing a public meeting
And could never remember our names. 'Let's see,
You must be Eva's youngest,' he said to me.
'What's your name? Alan?' He didn't even seem to know
That my mother's proper name was Mother,
Not Eva, which sounded strange and disrespectful.

Then, to my father's barely concealed merriment,
At the next election Lady Diana Cooper,
Wife of Duff, the Tory candidate, descended
Upon Oldham, dea ex machina,
Helping the women hang their washing out,
Cuddling infants, eating salted chips and vinegar
With her fingers for photographers and pressmen.
Her calculated charm and high-born glamour
Mesmerised mills and cobbled streets and terraces,
Row after row, leaving winded Uncle Jack
Plodding far behind on polling day, and Duff
Triumphant. Aunt Sissie never forgave her.
'That woman,' she would seethe, long after Uncle Jack
Had found a safer seat and, Oldham forgotten,
Duff Cooper climbed through Paris towards his peerage.

Because I was the youngest of the tribe,
Cousins by the score included, and 'delicate'
As the saying went in those days, Aunt Sissie
Always favoured me, bringing me small treats

And taking me back with her to Uncle Jack's
Sometimes when he was not at home. Yet I could never quite
Return the same affection that she showed to me.
Kneeling by the bed to say my prayers at night
Frightened me, it seemed so solemn and so cold.
And Todmorden, despite its cricket ground
(Cricket was my passion then) was gloomy
And forbidding, sunless in its gorge. I was always
Glad to go back home, and often let it show,
Finicky, ungrateful monster that I was.

For herself, Aunt Sissie never repined,
But small and fiercely independent,
Suffered in silence what she had to suffer,
Which was much. She went to her grave as quietly
As she had lived, giving no trouble. I learnt then
She had been christened Mary Ellen, and Sissie
Was only her familiar name. But to me
She will always be Aunt Sissie, her memory
Growing brighter, brighter with the years.

FAMILY TREE

Good mixer, matey, never doubting himself
Or his welcome, he turns up everywhere,
Old Adam, knowing the world is made of the same stuff
That fashioned him: greedy, lecherous, deceitful, sly,
And crower on small dungheaps, whom envy gnaws

Of bigger cocks on mightier middens, those
That grab the fattest grubs and pull the choicest birds.
You will meet him any Saturday in winter
Shoulder to shoulder crammed on draughty terraces,
Flat caps, raw faces, fags and boozy breath,

Aggression roaring out of 50 thousand throats ...
Ah, beg pardon, Sir, I hadn't seen you
Standing there, listening and looking on
And didn't quite catch what you said to me.
I said: you seem to know him pretty well—

On second thoughts, considering the likeness,
Not the most difficult of all hard things to do.

BEGINNINGS AND ENDS

It's the women mostly who get the worst of things,
With screams and groans bringing us to bloody birth, then
Suckling, cleansing us through all the nappied greed
Of infancy. Fifty years on,
Sagging like sacked potatoes, their offspring fled,
Observe them out of disillusioned habit
Tending the drooling wrecks that once were men.

AFTERNOON IN EARLY MARCH: EAST BELFAST

Pale sunlight gilds a windy sky,
Smoke-smudged at the edges. In Strandtown
And Ballyhackamore young wives
Waggle their little bottoms briskly
In and out of shops, their babies
Snug in prams. Loitering from school
In twos or threes satchelled children
Invade silent avenues
While big boys whistle past on bicycles
To swoop through garden gates. From distant docks
A siren sounds. Lights here and there
Begin to prick the dusk; and homes
In hundreds prepare contentedly for tea.

SEA AND STARS

I walk along the dunes. A westering sun
Flings spears of light across the mountains' crests,
Then falters, fades as shadows swathe the shore
And turf-smoke from the houses round the bay
Spirals into crisp, still air. It is the hour
Virgil knew and Sappho, when Hesperus
Draws creatures home, and glinting warmth within,
Small comforts, benedictions of the hearth
Beckon the stranger brushing like a moth
Past lighted windows. Watching my world
Lurch into autumn once again and drift
Beneath the snowstorm of the stars, I trudge
Towards the night where you have gone, a gull's
Far cry engulfed now in the shades and silence

Out at sea, yet echoing among the cliffs,
The sunless desolations of the heart.

ABSENTEE

A sudden clamour splits my skull. I reach
Out of bed to silence the alarm. Time
To get up, assume a morning face,
Rejoin the world. Instead I fall
After the nightmares, the sweating and the panic
Into deep slumber. The human race
Won't miss me. What is it after all,
This peace, if not a dry run for my funeral?

APPRECIATION, NOTES & INDEX

Norman Dugdale: A Personal Appreciation

Norman Dugdale, an Englishman, was born in Burnley in Lancashire in 1921, and lived in Belfast for more than half his life, a civil servant in the Northern Ireland Office, and for fourteen years until his retirement, Permanent Secretary of the Department of Health and Social Services. A distinguished career. At the same time he was pursuing quietly, almost secretly, hidden from his colleagues, his second career as a poet.

His poems cover a wide range of subjects, but a constant theme running through his work is his feeling for his adopted country, Northern Ireland, its towns and villages, countryside, and its men and women.

Norman described himself as "what the Greeks used to call a 'metic', a resident alien who enjoys the privilege of living and working in the city but who can never aspire to, or ever be granted, the full rights and responsibilities of citizenship." An outsider maybe, an observer from the sidelines. And yet his poems about Ulster are as perceptive of this troubled Province as any native-born might write. He expresses this poignantly in the poem 'Apparition' where a young republican with a "pale mad face" curses him viciously and yells to him 'Get to fuck out of Ulster!':

> Well over twice his age, I had lived here,
> Worked here, longer by far than my assailant,
> This was home…
> And yet it was the sting
> Of truth within his venom stopped me short.
> For him and his kind I am the enemy
> To be driven out, the scapegoat for all sins
> Whose going will bring peace and brotherhood
> Throughout the land. So they say, killing the while
> Those they call their countrymen who happen still
> To disagree.
> What kinship can I claim
> With the dissenters then? ...
> A stubborn race, their virtues out of fashion,
> Who will memorialise them now
> That Hewitt's dead, and I am a metic in their midst?

This poem comes from Norman's last book *Limbo*, published in 1991. However, he was much more than an outsider looking in. There is one further personal aspect of Norman Dugdale's which I feel must be taken into account when considering his poetry. As well as running the Health and Social Services Department, he himself had frequent recourse to the service he administered. Over many years he was dogged by ill-health which had meant many visits to specialists and several periods in hospital.

'A Question of Identity' describes one such experience, and there are several other poems or references in poems recalling in a matter-of-fact, laconic manner his hospitalisation. But the poem, 'Running Repairs', the title poem of his third book is the most important as it sets out his defiant attitude to his health problems. It is a discussion with a doctor about "a makeshift minor op":

'A proper job, of course,
Would not only take much longer but
Would call for general anaesthesia
Which is not recommended in your case'.

And the poem continues:

Not recommended in my case...? H'm, old
Bangers can't be choosers, I suppose.
And anyway it isn't far from here
To the knacker's yard. Oh, very well then: just
So long as you can keep me on the road.

A number of the poems carry an undercurrent of anxiety about sickness, about ageing, about death, about personal relationships. One gets the impression that Norman looked at life, in its many facets, with a wary eye.

Norman Dugdale became part of the Ulster poetry scene, round about 1963, when he was invited by Philip Hobsbaum to join 'The Group', a number of poets got together by Hobsbaum, an Englishman and a poet who was a lecturer in the English Department of Queen's University. 'The Group', a fairly amorphous collection of poets and would-be poets, met once a week in Hobsbaum's flat where one member would read his work which was then discussed and dissected by the rest, with no holds barred. Norman joined 'The Group' with some trepidation since in his official way of life he had had little contact with writers. But he had had some poems published, and when these were brought to his attention by John Smith, then editor of *Poetry Review*, Hobsbaum, rightly, considered he should be invited to join 'The Group'.

Norman wrote a full and fascinating account of his first meeting. He slipped unobtrusively into a packed room, where most of those present seemed to be much younger than he was, many of them students. The reader was Seamus Heaney, as yet unpublished. The ensuing discussion was provocative and stimulating.

There were other names he knew but had not previously met. He was hooked and became a regular attender.

It was a time of peace, cooperation between Catholics and Protestants and optimism in Northern Ireland; an atmosphere where poetry flourished, and 'The Group's' members too. But it could not last. In 1966 Hobsbaum left for a post at Glasgow University. Then, after a year in America, Seamus Heaney returned to become convenor, but not for long. He moved south with his family. And the Troubles flared up again and were getting more violent and disastrous. Gradually 'The Group' disintegrated: "There was no-one left", Norman has written, "with the time, the standing or the heart to continue." He himself had given up going to meetings because of pressure of work.

As I wrote earlier, Norman regarded Belfast as his home but he still recalled his English roots. Two long poems provide the evidence for that. 'Haven Street' paints an affectionate picture of his family, in Haven Street, Burnley, in the 30s and 40s. Uncle Henry, who "always wore his cap indoors/On top of a knitted woollen helmet which/Covered his ears and chin" and Aunt Bertha (also lovingly described later in 'What's Wrong with Aberystwyth?'):

> Somehow Aunt Bertha
> Managed on their dole; patched, darned, scoured the Co-ops
> For bargains, kept the place neat, sent cross-words in
> Sometimes to *Tit-Bits* or *John Bull*, never won.
> ...
> Whenever we
> Visited as children (which wasn't often),
> Aunt Bertha beamed at us, pressed us to bread, tinned
> Salmon, tea ...

And then there was Aunt Annie "jingling her pendant ear-rings with/An air of languor and disdain. Aunt Annie,/You see was a ruined woman."

A wonderful picture of a working-class family in the 30s, which also brings in the poet's loved father.

> After the War—my father dead, Aunt Annie
> Too—my wife and I called once or twice, newly
> Married. His stammer worse, Uncle Henry hid
> In his corner, trying to conceal the white
> Bristles that spiked his chin. Aunt Bertha, beaming,

Told us about my father as a lad—how
Mathematics hoisted him out of the mill:
How he filled a drawer with silver, kept it so
For everyone to help themselves; came home then
At all hours, whistling up again by five ...

The one day we heard from home that she was dead—
A fortnight later, Uncle Henry too, a
Hundred pounds in notes stuffed underneath their bed.

In the last stanza, the nephew and son, from his well-appointed
office, "My carpet runs from wall/To wall; fresh flowers grace a side-
table; thick/Velvet curtains reach down to the floor..." looks sadly
back to those earlier days, regretting his lost chances.

In the second long family poem, 'A Winter Journey', Norman
recalls his grief at the death of his father: "Twenty-five years ago I
hiccuped sobs/And snivelled through my father's funeral." He
then moves on to his mother's death and his memories of her:

What have I brought you now, so shrunk
By death I cannot bear
To look on you in that cold room
Or others to look? A pair

Of gold-rimmed specs (my first
In middle-age) to make
You laugh: the jacket of a book
(My only child, late born) which I

Had named for you, that you might die
Knowing something fathered for your sake.

Then he takes the plane "For Ireland. So the fixed star gone,/Of my
triangulated life, I grope/Towards my landfall".

His landfall, his home now, is Ireland. In 'Travelling Westward',
he questions and rejects whether he should have left England:

Travelling westward this day, through the shires,
Worcestershire, Gloucestershire and Somerset,
Timbered, cricketing counties...

I think
Of that farther island in the west ...

I should have left her long since, settled here

Where I belong. Not now. What should I do
Without her ...

I have grown old
In her toils ...

There are other poems about journeys by plane, train, boat, in
which the traveller makes it clear he is coming home to Belfast.
'Single Ticket' is one; 'Crossings' is another: a journey on the boat
train and then the ship, a long, very descriptive poem in two
distinctive styles.

In 'Small Hours', he is on a plane at night looking down on a
troubled Belfast:

Suddenly the cratered city
Opens below, glittering there
Like a gigantic jewelled drinking-bowl,
And you slither down to find

Its doors slammed shut, blinds drawn
Against the stranger, its streets deserted
Though traffic-lights blink madly at road-ends.
And always you feel you are being watched

From alleyways and corners, stalked
As you halt or hesitate
Within the maze. Next day
You recognise the place as home,

Crumpled, mud-stained and familiar
As some old suit, camouflage
Which only half conceal from mind and eye
The sub-culture of murder and atrocity

Flourishing below.

The most direct reference to Belfast as home comes in 'Night
Ferry', in his second book, *Corncrake in October*. Arriving off the ferry
to a wet Belfast morning:

Wall slogans run like wet mascara
Down gable ends. The terraces
Wear jilted looks, deserted
In the morning, swollen-eyed,

But last night's rain has rinsed the streets
Of last night's vomit, last night's blood.
'Where to, sir?' asks the taximan. 'Home,'
I say. 'Where's that?' 'Home's here, ' I say, 'for good.'

In one poem, 'The Farther Shore', about a journey back to
Burnley, Dugdale ponders whether he was right to have left:

Too late I reach
Towards lives I almost touch, they seem so near,
Yet now recede from, faster every year.

This poem comes from his first book, *A Prospect of the West*,
dedicated to his mother. The poem about her death, 'A Winter
Journey', is the last long poem in *Corncrake in October*. Is it at that
point that the strings tying him to his home in Burnley were broken,
and Belfast he now thinks of as home? I quote again these lines from
'A Winter Journey'.

So the fixed star gone
Of my triangulated life, I grope
Towards my landfall

Norman's many poems about the Irish countryside, about its
towns (and about English towns and country too), capture exactly
the scene he is describing, with a precise use of words, a telling
phrase, so that at once there is a visual picture before your eyes.
In 'Kerry', his first poem, when he was seriously starting to write
while on holiday in Kerry with his wife, Mary, to whom he has written
some poignant love poems, there is a perfect visual description:
"Here Ireland thrusts a great arthritic fist/Into the green Atlantic…"
Or 'November Afternoon':

A sour wind
Slouches off the lough, with knife in hand
Skins children's faces hurrying home
From school…

Or from 'Aubade', a poem about bomb-strewn Belfast: "Now
buses jerk/Red corpuscles down clotted streets/Where suburbs
cough to consciousness."
Turning to the natural world, there are many beautifully crafted
poems, long and short. Picture this scene from a lovely poem
'Northern Spring':

Whins blaze along the coast
From Fair Head now to Fanad—

And violets in the ditch and primroses,

Small trumpeters of resurrection,
On either bank. It is the whins'
Fierce shout, though, lifts the heart, war-bands
Rallied here against the sap

And siege of time: their sudden
Glory searing gullies, haloing the hills.

Other enchanting 'nature' poems include 'Michaelmas':

Above a shining sea honeysuckle
Flares now through the hedgerows. By bank, by ditch
Bright with campions and foxgloves, bees
Weave their delicate dance, and purple vetch

Hangs tremulous...

And 'Salmon Leap: County Mayo' with salmon like "Black torpedoes
locked/On target, coming home". And I must mention here the
poems about a 'Robin Among Summer Visitors'—"Connoisseur of
bread crumbs and grilled bacon rind .../Red kerchief slashed,
pirate-fashion round his neck"; and the mole ('Anarchist'):

Sapper, snorting under sleep, furiously
Detonating smooth suburban lawns: small
Sharp-snouted saboteur...

Then there is the spider in 'Natural History', "When ignorance
and folly squat/Like toads on top, arachnids scuttle clear". And
talking of toads what about "That clammy toad with popped/Green
stare and palpitating chin/Who squatted at table, belching, blown/
So tight he could not budge..." from a strange little poem 'On a
Recent Happy Event'.

Norman's use of exact but unexpected words to build up a vivid
picture is particularly effective in 'Littoral', a long ambitious poem
in four parts. In the wild west coast of Ireland, the poet takes his dog
for a walk in fierce wind and rain. He looks at the mountains:

Heads down

Their pelted faces trickling rain
Under black sou'-westers of storm cloud,
The mountains haul the cabled road
That whips and writhes between us and the main.

Later in a "night thick with stars", he studies the constellations,
the terrier

Snuffling in the ditch, startling
A bird from sleep, beasts coughing in a byre—
Bird, beasts, dog, man, mere
Specks of carbon capering
(Not at will) in figure of the dance,
The mad molecular quadrille ...

He then muses on how man came to "this cold melancholy
shore": "Here Norman, Saxon, figures in a mist/Loomed briefly
large before/They were sucked into the bog ... "
    And in the final stanza nothing is left "as the days/Melt like
footprints in wet sand".
    To return to the more specifically 'nature' poems, it is noticeable
how frequently whins (gorse) make an appearance. Breaking away
from a sometimes sombre atmosphere as in 'Littoral', it is clear that
Norman loves the whins and the bright gold they display. In
'Donegal', he writes about "this land .../Is Midas-touched by
spring,/Its ragged banks and boreens/Burgeoning gold". And,
most of all, in 'At Saul', there is almost a shout of joy for spring:

Rouse me, March, from this long torpor
Now daffodils at muster blow
Their bugles in the dells and whins
Break cover in the gullies, roar
Up bank and boreen, fire drumlins,
Set byres ablaze ...

    The English poems have the same power to bring the scene to
life: 'Pennines' or 'Dalesmen in Craven', with their lovely sounding
words which trip off the tongue, or most poignantly, 'Higher
Hodder', where the sounds and sights of nature mingle with
recollections of Norman's grandfather who at "eighty fished this
stream/Walking the green heart still of grace/On mornings like
this morning thick/And drowsy with the musk of may."
    Here, as in so many poems, nostalgically he looks back in middle
age to the past.

As a resident of Ulster for over forty years, Norman Dugdale lived through times of turbulence, of bombs, of death. In his 1992 Christmas card he told me that Bryson House, a cross-community, multi-purpose charity of which he was chairman, had been badly damaged twice that year by massive explosions. He wrote "but there were no casualties. Thanks to our resilient and resolute staff, both Roman Catholic and Protestant, drawn from all parts of the city, including the hard-line ghettoes we were soon back in business. This too is standard form". Inevitably, there are poems about 'the Troubles'. 'Apparition', from his last book, which I have already commented on; 'Nocturne', contrasting "the Green and Orange with their god-crazed eyes,/Despair and rage at riot in their blood", with the moon which " ... steps free scouring rooftops white,/ Cascading through stone chasms, silently/Flooding the fronded city with salt light."

'Marches' tells of a drive through a menacing night:

After dark, it is best to keep moving—
Not too fast, for the roads
Wriggle through hills, slithering past hedge and ditch
And the next bend may conceal a few stray cows
Or a blown bridge or ambush. But if you can,
Keep moving, headlamps drilling the night.

The long poem, in two parts, 'In Memoriam G.B. Newe' is written to an old friend. In 1972 from his hospital bed Dugdale expresses his admiration for his friend's refusal to accept violence as a viable solution.

You knew the cost
Of not stampeding with the rest
Or hurling a bomb or abuse
Was ostracism at the best—
At worst a bullet in the back.
But 'Charity comes first,' you said
'Not justice. Justice without charity
Will never reconcile or make us whole'.

And ten years later, he is in Cushendall

To pay my last respects beside your grave.
This was your place, and these your people
Who welcome me a stranger to their rite
With rough warm handshakes bonding common grief.

With a lighter touch and on a charmingly optimistic note, 'After the Bombing' describes two young lovers, oblivious of the destruction around them, looking for somewhere private:

> They came hurrying down the street, laughing
> Together and smiling at each other,
> Then paused at the kerb to snatch a kiss...
> Love and life are indestructible.

So far I have written about Norman Dugdale's poetry which deals with his own personal experiences: his family, his Belfast home, his travels, his communication with nature. But that is only one side to his character. He was a scholar of wide-ranging academic qualities, immensely well-read, with a knowledge of Italian, Latin and Greek; many of these interests are to be found in his poems. He had special affection and respect for the Greek poet, C.P. Cavafy, who lived from 1863 to 1933. A Greek quotation from Cavafy prefaces both *Running Repairs* and *Limbo*. Cavafy was a civil servant under the British, described by Norman as "a quintessential Alexandrian". He paints his picture in 'The Last Alexandrian':

> I rummage through his multiple disguises
> Searching for the essence of the man
> This Greek turned Englishman turned Greek again,
> Clerk who drudged for thirty years by day
> In the Third Circle of the Irrigation Office
> With starched high collar, sober suit, pince-nez
> And carefully protruding cuffs: cautious, mean
> Cutting his cigarettes in half ...

and yet an outrageous libertine by night, fusing all that experience into "verse/Shot through with glory like an icon,/Sombre, elegiac, serene".

In notes at the end of *Limbo*, Norman writes that Cavafy is difficult to translate into English "without disrupting his rhythm or distorting his tone". He has himself written translations or versions of two Cavafy poems. One is 'Theodotos'. In the other, 'In a Large Greek Colony: 200 BC', the conversational style is brilliantly used to show the irritation of the resident civil servants at the 'political reformers' brought in to interfere in the smooth running of the colony.

From the Italian, Norman Dugdale had translated a sonnet by Ugo Foscolo, a poet and patriot, born in 1778: 'A Self-Portrait' and a very unflattering self-portrait at that and there is a delightful translation of Horace's Ode to Venus, where the poet begs the goddess to leave him alone—"I am getting on for fifty after all/And have almost forgotten the drill"—and turn her attention to "Paulus Maximus/That brilliant young lawyer." But typically Horace is loath to give up his goddess:

> If she should vanish
> All will go dead within, or worse (far worse)
> Empty years stretch out while underneath
> The thickening crust the sterile fires still burn.

All Norman's translations, unlike so many in this genre, do not read as if the words have been painstakingly transferred from one language to another but have a flowing rhythmical style all their own.

The classical world is a constant theme running through so much of his work, and in particular a deep love for Greece, ancient and modern. Some poems are straight-forward accounts of Greek myths.

There is 'Perseus' confronting through glass the writhing snakes of Medusa's hair. And in the next poem 'Galatea to Pygmalion', Galatea rejoices that she is now a living woman and pours scorn on Pygmalion's revulsion at what he has created. Three poems describe Odysseus' travels from Troy to Ithaca, 'Sea Change', 'Scheria' and 'Ithaca', in which he talks of his home-coming.

> Home? Is this truly Ithaca
> Again?...
>   What gifts
> Have I or any brought this stony land,
> Save empty hands, a few tall tales?

Several poems with a classical background are used to paint a more universal statement about human barbarism and human impotence in the face of it. This is the subject of 'A Statement is Expected Shortly'. 'Polycrates' Ring' is a sharp lesson in cynicism in the face of flattery and superstition. And most strongly in 'Medizers', Greeks who sided with Xerxes and the Persians, believing this was in their own self-interest, we are reminded that:

> They are still around today, realists
> Counselling compromise and caution,
> Men comfortably off with much to lose
> Like their predecessors in that hot, dry spring.
> Now, informed observers everywhere commend
> Their moderation and good sense.

'The Commissars Confirm Their Shortlist' is in the same vein:
how the Establishment looks after its own and to hell with the rest
"nameless, undefined/Except by what they're not: unplaced/Among
the halt, the lame, the blind". This anger against the Establishment
is also turned against the philistines, against those, for example,
who fail to appreciate the beauty of Greece and her islands. There
are some fine poems which bring out Norman's own emotions
during a holiday in Greece. They include some of his most lyrical
verses. Take these lines from 'Thasus':

> Morning sparkles in the bay
> Like sapphire in a clasp of pearls. Boats
> Chuckle now ashore. This
> Island in antiquity
> Thrived on gold from Thrace and wine
> Famous for its excellent bouquet.

'Thasos' is full of the beauty of the place. There is the climb up
a "steep hillside" and "a vertiginous descent".

> We come back once more to the square
> Where we stop for drinks.
> And that is all, except that I

> Am drunk already, having no need of wine ...

This poem is from Norman's second book, *Corncrake in October*,
a collection which features prominently poems about Greece or
refers to Greek subjects. A Greek couplet used in the volume
demonstrates Dugdale's passion for the classical world: "but at that
sight my heart stood long astonished/for never sapling shot from
earth so fair."

They must have been written in a burst of creativity after a visit to
that lovely part of the world.

Sadly any visit to Greece has its darker side: the supremely
ignorant tourist lambasted in several poems. Here in 'Not in the
Brochure':

> By plane this time, by coach they come,
> Relentless as the horsemen of Attila,
> Swarming south to cluster on the coast
> Where, methodically taking off their clothes,
> They settle to the serious business
> Of acquiring a suntan...

'Scholar Emeritus' contrasts the dignified, elderly scholar "high on the gangway" trying to catch the interest of "the sunbathers sprawled below" in Sappho as the boat sails towards Lesbos. Norman Dugdale's hatred of and despair about philistines, whether ignorant tourists or bigots of all kinds, runs through many of his poems. It is perhaps justified to describe him here, in these often quite short poems, as the observer on the sidelines, mercilessly dissecting, with a dry wit, people, institutions, ways of life, whose materialistic values are so different from his own. In 'How to Become an Alexandrian', the idle, self-seeking academic is viciously taken to pieces:

You lecture in English. This confers prestige
(It is better to lecture than to teach)
And creates a presumption of knowledge.

Other succinct little poems, for example 'Leader of Men', 'Pillar of Society', 'Diplomatic Reception', and the longer 'Provincia Deserta' all attack the complacency of the men at the top.

In another strain, several of these witty, cynical poems are directed against himself. At 'Staff Party', thinking to impress a pretty woman, "I clowned a while and told my favourite jokes", only to find she is more excited to hear about Smyth—"him of the wheezy chest,/The woollen cardigan and grizzled head". 'New Management' finds him going back to an office building he thought he knew well, to search out an old colleague, only to be told by an arrogant woman that there is no-one of that name and to get out or she will have him thrown out.

Another recurring theme is that of growing old with all its drawbacks. Two bitter little poems are entitled 'Age' and this attitude is best summed up in 'Gerousia'. On 'the first bright day of spring, the old men come out

Hobbling on their sticks into the park
To warm old bones...
In coats and caps and scarves. 'Bit chilly still',
I say, nodding as I pass. They grunt or nod
In turn, sparing speech. A year or two and I
Shall take my seat in their laconic council.

That describes the present and the possibly melancholy future. In contrast, these are poems setting out scenes from the poet's past: 'Age of Heroes', a visit to the cinema as a boy on a wet, winter Saturday, watching a film "where bad men always bit the dust"; or

'School Photograph',—the head prefect "I recollect/Chiefly now
his arrogance and vanity"; or 'Peripeteia', the weakling whom
schoolmates nicknamed 'Pansy' who years later, come the war, was
encountered

> ... sporting a pipe
> And a smashing girl and wings and medal ribbons
> And gold-leaf on his cap. 'Er... hello.' I said...

> He waved and passed on. He had forgotten me.
> No doubt, subfusc in civvies anyway.

I hope that already I have illustrated the range and variety of
Dugdale's poetry covering so many subjects. What is particularly
outstanding was his love of language, his love of words and the
sound of words—exactly the right word, the right *sound*, in the right
place. He plays perfectly with place names in 'Proper Names':

> Ballydehob, for example
> Couldn't be anywhere else
> Or other than Ballydehob;
> Or Skibbereen name anything

> But Skibbereen...

> But Dingle, Bantry, Baltimore—
> Old traffickers by south and west
> Salt-blistered—lure with sea-mew's cry: sprawl
> In lethargy, their timbers sprung.

In other poems he uses staccato, noisy-sounding words to get the
effect he wants; in 'Inner City', here is how he brings to life the wind

> How it blows...
> On silent quays, rattles windows, smashes slates,
> Rolls dustbins round backyards, lifts curtains, slams
> Doors shut.

This meticulous use of the sound of words is illustrated most
brilliantly in the sonnet 'Trading Station', another with a classical
theme. The sailor limps "ashore in this Phoenician town"

> ... where heat bangs down
> Like a dustbin lid at noon, clamping the din,

The sizzling flies, fish heads, straw, and smells
Of rotting fruit and garbage tight within.

The town is clearly visible in the heat. But in the last six lines of
the sonnet, the mood changes; all is peaceful, somnolent:

Through the silence then of shuttered afternoon
Gold filters onto golden skin
And shadowed eyes. He spends his manhood here
Whose business lies in distant waters, beached
In this creek of time, her salted mouth,
The scented whorls and sea-lift of her hair.

I have quoted almost all of this beautiful sonnet because it
encapsulates so many of Norman Dugdale's themes: a classical
theme, rattling staccato words depicting noise, a lyrical flow of
words describing beauty, a golden light. Another lovely poem with
the same use of language, part-nature, part-classical, part-personal
is 'Persephone'. This scrupulous choice of the right word, the exact
phrase, runs through all Norman's work.

Also to be found permeating his poetry is a clear philosophical
vein. Many of the longer, more abstract poems question accepted
values, unprincipled self-seekers, the whole attitude of the
materialistic world in which we live. Some of them chronicle
personal disappointment and a sense of disillusion with himself and
life in general. The title poem of his first book, 'A Prospect of the
West', is a clear example. Others are 'Against Abstractions' and
'Reasons of State'. In 'Columkille' a poem in three parts, an account
of tracking down an eagle over several years becomes a musing over
human attitudes. 'White Church at Ballintoy' the penultimate
poem in the collection, is again descriptive and personal. The poet
talks of the village and its surroundings, he enters the church, and
then the poem ends on a desolate, intensely personal note—too sad
to quote here.

Possibly 'Moralities', a long poem in couplets and divided into
four sections, sets out most exactly Norman Dugdale's attitude to
life—youth, frustrating middle age, "a litter of disappointed hopes".
It ends, one has to believe, on an up-beat note:

The worst
Is to be humped off pick-a-back by self...

And dumped then in the midst of desolation,
Utterly alone, where there is neither beast

Nor birdsong, no leaf, no shade, no water,
And no redemption save

Through the miraculous daring
(Is it only a mirage,

The flickering horizon?)
Of the frail, unbidden dove.

It cannot be denied that in so much of his life, the fates have
treated the poet harshly: his Ulster environment, his health, his
disenchantment with the Establishment. But there was always hope,
and the will to pull through.

The last poem in this collection is 'Limbo', the title poem of
Dugdale's last book. It is a sad poem, giving the impression that
there is nothing to look forward to. To my mind that air of defeatism
is wrong and untypical if one looks back over the whole range of his
work. A far more accurate view of his life and work is to be found in
the first poem in his first book, *A Prospect of the West*, and the first
poem in this collection. Entitled 'One and Many', it begins:

Lord, let me now and then forget
The bag of bones I lug round yet ...

and it ends:

So, by gifts of touch and sight
Walking my world, may I pass through
All false identities to grasp the true.

Everyone who reads through Norman Dugdale's poems, as I have
done now many times, will understand at once how he did just that.
In a long life, he passed through all false identities and grasped the
true. He was a fine man and a fine poet.

Elizabeth Thomas
10th January 1997

Elizabeth Thomas is a reviewer and critic and a former literary editor of
Tribune, *where she published several of Norman Dugdale's poems.*

Author's Notes

A Self-Portrait (p.46)
Freely translated from the sonnet 'Il Proprio Ritratto' by Ugo Foscolo (1778-1827), Italian poet and patriot, who ended his days in exile in England.

The Last Alexandrian (p.64)
C.P. Cavafy (1863-1827), Greek poet, civil servant under the British, and quintessential Alexandrian.

In a Large Greek Colony: 200 BC (p. 165)
Cavafy's translators rarely attempt to produce his rhymes, presumably because they are so difficult to carry over into English without disrupting his rhythm or distorting his tone. John Mavrogordato is the exception that proves the rule. His unrhymed version of Cavafy are among the most accomplished I know; but when he rhymes, he does so with an exuberance quite out of keeping with Cavafy's habitual restraint and gravity of address. Cavafy is supremely a poet of statement and irony, not of vivid images or arresting metaphor. (In this respect he fails to conform to contemporary Western notions of what poetry should be.) His rhymes are exact but unobtrusive, reinforcing meaning without drawing attention to technique. It is, of course, impossible fully to reflect in English either Cavafy's inimitable voice or his versification, much less to echo his multiple ironies. Nevertheless, rhyme is important part of his armoury, not to be ignored. Unemphatic devices, such as pararhyme, near rhyme, rhyming on final *y* to mimic Cavafy's frequent rhymes on unstressed *ee*, are, it seems to me, legitimate means of approximating his effects.

Cretan Mantinada (p. 109)
The mantinada is a traditional verse form in the island of Crete, consisting of a rhymed couplet, often, but not always, with satiric intent.

Medizers (p. 115)
Greeks who sided with the Persians (Medes) when Xerxes, the Persian king, invaded Greece with massive force in 480 BC.

Gerousia (p. 120)
The council of elders at Sparta which had large jurisdiction in political affairs and formed the highest executive committee of the state.

Publisher's note

This collected edition of Norman Dugdale's poems was initiated shortly before the poet's death in October,1995. While this collection contains all of his poems published in book form plus a nearly complete new and untitled volume, it was impossible to provide accurate dates for the earlier poems. It was decided, therefore, that, in order to avoid inaccuracy, the first date on the cover should refer to the publication of his debut volume, *A Prospect of the West* (1970). In order to clarify some of the poems, all the author's notes from previous volumes have been reprinted. In the *New and Uncollected Poems*, 'Ancestry' (p. 132) and 'Family Tree' (p. 144) are versions of the same poem: it was decided to include both versions as the author's wishes were unknown. Finally, for typographical and design reasons, it was impossible to include section breaks and dedications of individual volumes. *A Prospect of the West* was dedicated 'For My Mother' and *Limbo* (1991) was dedicated 'For Mary'.

TITLE INDEX

A Memorial for My Sister *129*
A Narrow Place *29*
A Question of Identity *34*
A Statement
  is Expected Shortly *76*
A Study in Sepia *57*
A Toast *128*
A Winter Journey *67*
A Woman of Nazareth *130*
Absentee *146*
After the Bombing *86*
Afternoon in Early March:
  East Belfast *145*
Against Abstraction *27*
Age *91*
Age *109*
Age of Heroes *112*
All for Hecuba *55*
An Enemy *28*
An Exorcism *33*
Anarchist *42*
Ancestry *132*
Anglican Church: West Cork *4*
Apocalypse *62*
Apparition *118*
At Saul *87*
Aubade *49*
Aunt Sissie *142*
Autopsy on the
  Fourth Decade *44*

Back to the Basics *79*
Back Water *54*
Ballymacarrett Blues:
  Summer 1994 *132*
Beginnings and Ends *145*
Belfast *7*
Bog *41*
But for Your Gifts *85*

Camouflage *131*
Candles *81*
Celtic Bard,
  Burgher's Wife *120*
Christmas Eve *141*
Clerk's Tale *47*
Closed Shop *130*
Columkille *74*
Corncrake in October *58*
Cretan Mantinada *109*
Crossings *116*

Dalesmen in Craven *59*
Daybreak *93*
Definitions *46*
Diplomatic Reception *92*
Disciplinary Case *45*
Dolphins *63*
Domestic Interior *121*
Donegal *101*
Downham Revisited *16*
Dublin *6*

Easter in Craven *12*
Elder Statesman *101*
Encounters *89*
End of Season *77*
End of the Affair *138*
Epiphany *140*
Evensong *31*
Family Tree *144*
Final Act *107*
Fire Risk *43*
Five Cretan Mantinades *138*
For Better For Worse *20*
Frontier Incident *23*

Galatea to Pygmalion *26*
Gerousia *120*

Glenarm *94*
Great Portland Street *19*
Grief *83*

Half-Remembered Things *127*
Hallowe'en *107*
Harvest *140*
Haven Street *13*
Haworth *12*
High Hodder *84*
Homage to the Bard *108*
Home for Christmas *82*
How to Become
  an Alexandrian *84*
Hurstwood *60*

In a Large Greek Colony:
  200 BC *105*
In Memoriam G.B. Newe *89*
Inner City *106*
Insomnia *119*
Ithaca *66*

Journeys End *81*

Kerry *4*

Landfall *10*
Landscape in Winter *142*
Lares *48*
Last Night *115*
Leader of Men *109*
Lent *75*
Limbo *123*
Lines for an Old Lady *9*
Littoral *49*
Long-Distance
  Coach Station *104*
Louis MacNeice *9*
Lovers *107*
Lower Order *139*

Maker *135*
Man of Property *136*

Marches *45*
Mason *83*
Medical Ward *134*
Medizers *115*
Metamorphosis *119*
Michaelmas *82*
Moralities *96*
Mr. Cavafy's Byzantine
  Archon Versifying
  in His Exile *114*
Natural History *110*
Nekuia *55*
New Management *102*

Night-Ferry *55*
No Second Troy? *61*
Nocturne *26*
Northern Spring *47*
Not in the Brochure *61*
November Afternoon *49*

Old Man Sitting
  in the Park *110*
Olympic Games *118*
On a Recent Happy Event *29*
One and Many *3*
One of the Boys *141*
Overture and Beginners *121*

Pantechnicon *77*
Pavane for the 'Forty-Five *19*
Pennines *11*
Peripeteia *58*
Persephone *8*
Perseus *25*
Personal Appearance *3*
Pillar of Society *80*
Place and Time *54*
Planter *139*
Polonius Complains *117*
Polycrates' Ring *82*
Poor Fitz *20*
Pre-Retirement Course *111*
Prelude *133*

Problem Family 53
Progeny 109
Prolegomena 39
Proper Names 52
Prospect of the West 30
Provincia Deserta 78

Queene and Huntresse 25
Quis Multa Gracilis ... ? 79

Reasons of State 15
Recluse 53
Rector 137
Remembrance
  of Things Past 57
Remorse 120
Retrospect 27
Ribblesdale 113
Robin Among
  Summer Visitors 102
Rue Lepsius 136
Running Repairs 96

Salmon-Leap: Co. Mayo 43
Satan's Advice 117
Scheria 64
Scholar Emeritus 65
Scholar in the Library 87
School Photograph 103
Scrapheap 133
Sea and Stars 145
Sea-Change 34
Seated King and Queen 48
Second-Hand Bookstall 88
Self-Portrait 46
Shipwrecked Mariner 92
Shoreditch 134
Shrouded Coast 101
Silence 98
Single Ticket 35
Small Hours 94
Some Notes
  for Impartial Observers 42
Souterrain 80

South Mancester Revisited 58
Specimen 93
Spirit of Place 73
St. James's, Piccadilly 113
Staff Party 118
Sunday Service 134
Swift 8

The Commissars Confirm
  their Short List 111
The Disposition
  of the Weather 22
The Farther Shore 17
The Last Alexandrian 64
The Other Kingdom 121
The Roundabout 142

Talking Head 109
Terminus 56
Thasos 65
Theodotos 95
Theologian 73
There are More Things 142
To an English Liberal,
  Ten Years On 89
To Venus 24
Tourist Season 18
Trading Station 110
Travelling Westward 86
Trivia 88
Tryst 103
Two in Connemara 5
Tynan 104

Visitation 77

Waste 52
What's Wrong
  with Aberystwyth? 110
White Church at Ballintoy 122

Young Man and Old 127

Zoo 122

OTHER POETRY TITLES

from

LAGAN PRESS

Robert Greacen
Collected Poems 1944-1994
introduced by the author
ISBN: 1 873687 55 9
176 pp, £5.95 pbk

"Greacen's is a voice that has been given too little heed in his native country. The poems run the gamut—one might also say the gauntlet—of human emotions and respond with the subtlest of sardonic satire, with the most suavely debonair urbanity and with an honest and sincerity that are totally disarming."

—Conleth Ellis, *Books Ireland*

"It is with shrewd observation, a fine Swiftian wit and considerable poetic control that Greacen views a modern society inhabited by ordinary people. He writes with an immediacy that is much sought after these days."

—Martin Booth, *British Book News*

For fifty years Robert Greacen has been one of the most distinctive voices in Irish poetry. From the political and aesthetic intensities of the neo-Romantic *One Recent Evening* (1944) and *The Undying Day* (1948), through the ironic and urbane satires of *A Garland for Captain Fox* (1975) and *Young Mr. Gibbon* (1979), to the autobiographical celebrations and elegies of his northern upbringing in *Carnival at the River* (1990), he has followed his own course outside the prevailing modes of poetic fashion. Yet unifying the poems is a belief in poetry and its ceaseless engagement with the self and the social world.

Gathering together all of his poetic output to the present day, *Robert Greacen: Collected Poems 1944-1994* stands as a testimoney to a unique sensibility in modern Irish poetry.

Winner of the *Irish Times* Literary Prize for Poetry 1995

Roy McFadden
Collected Poems 1943-1995
introduced by Philip Hobsbaum
ISBN: 1 873687 16 8/1 873 687 21 4
374 pp, £5.95 pbk/£25.00 hbk

Roy McFadden was born in Belfast in 1921. A co-editor of the influential *Rann* magazine, he is a major figure in the development of northern Irish poetry. He has published eight volumes, the latest being *After Seymour's Funeral* (Blackstaff Press, 1990). His *Selected Poems* appeared in 1982.

"McFadden belongs to that honourable tradition of poets who may trace descent from Horace: fastidious word-carvers, urban recorders of daily lives, followers of the golden mean ... A quiet voice more audible than all the shriekers shrieking together."
—Paul Durcan

"A fierce if seemingly diffident radical ... a consummate craftsman."
—Padraic Fiacc

"The most essential quality of his work is of a fastidious clarity of feeling which holds the mind and should command the attention of anyone interest in Irish poetry."
—Edna Longley

For more than half a century, Roy McFadden has been one of Ireland's leading poets. Over eight collections he has charted a fierce individualistic landscape in counterpoise to the civil disintegration of the north of Ireland. In 1950 he wrote: "Our roots travel widely and ignore boundaries and cultural geographical units. What we need is a way of life, personal, dignified and purposeful ... Rilke's sombre reflection is painfully relevant: *You must alter your life.*"

Introduced by Philip Hobsbaum, *Roy McFadden: Collected Poems 1943-1995* stands as a testimony to the artistic vitality of that quest.

Padraic Fiacc
Red Earth
ISBN: 1 873687 90 7
72 pp, £4.95 pbk

Red Earth is Padraic Fiacc's first new volume of poetry since his selected poems, *Ruined Pages*, was shortlisted for the *Irish Times* Literature Prize for Poetry in 1995, bringing to new critical and popular attention the most harrowing Irish poet of the century.

This volume, collecting poems written over four decades, draws on influences and concerns at the core of Fiacc's aesthetic—the darker elements of Celtic mythology which seep easily into the vexed environment of a contemporary and troubled Ireland in poetry thoroughly informed by the artist's alertness to European economy of expression.

Surprising, evocative, pungent and disconcerting, *Red Earth* exposes another deep dimension in this worrisome imagination, restoring a poet who has so often appeared out-of-kilter with the ethics of the time to the sombre mainstream of Irish verse.